Contents

Welcome to Amarna!

Egypt is a country with many fascinating stories to tell. From ancient history to life today, the people, places, buildings and traditions of Egypt have captured the imagination of the world.

This book explores one of the special places in Egypt – Amarna. Amarna was once a great city. Today it is the home of communities who lead modern lives next to (and sometimes on top of) the ancient ruins.

More than 25,000 people live in Amarna today in the towns of Tell Beni Amran (El-Till), El-Hagg Qandil, and El-Ammariyya. If you look carefully, in between the modern houses, schools, roads and farmland there are clues that tell us about a time when Amarna was the most important city in all of Egypt!

Amarna can be found about half way between the capital city of Cairo in the north and Luxor in the south. See if you can find Cairo, Amarna and Luxor on the map! Amarna is on the east bank of the great river Nile.

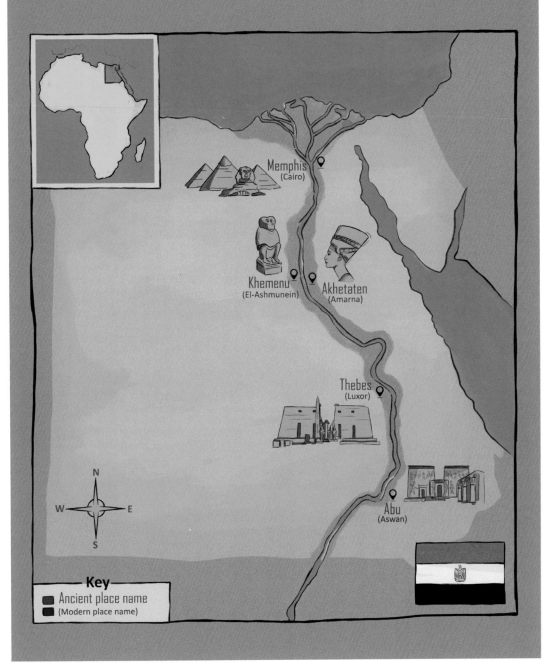

Memphis
(Cairo)

Khemenu
(El-Ashmunein)

Akhetaten
(Amarna)

Thebes
(Luxor)

Abu
(Aswan)

N
W   E
S

Key
Ancient place name
(Modern place name)

Over 3000 years ago Amarna had a different name. It was called Akhetaten. This is how Akhetaten was written in ancient Egyptian writing, which is called hieroglyphs.

Can you see how the first symbol on the left looks like the sun rising between two mountains? Akhetaten means 'Horizon of the Sun Disc' in ancient Egyptian: the mountain sign is the horizon (Akhet) and the signs to the right spell Aten (the sun).

The King (Pharaoh), Akhenaten, ordered the city to be built. At Akhetaten he started the world's first recorded religion to focus on just one god, a sun god, he called the Aten. He banned the other gods of ancient Egypt! To please the King, people came from all over Egypt to help build his new capital city out of mudbrick and stone. Akhenaten's wife, Nefertiti, and his family also moved to the new city to support the King. Life was focused on the worship of the sun god. Sculptors, scribes, builders, farmers, administrators and craftspeople were all needed.

Turn to the glossary page 56 to learn the meaning of the words written in **orange**!

Big open-air temples with beautiful sculptures and eye-catching art were at the heart of the city. It was a busy place and lots of work went into preparing offerings to the sun god at the temples. In a very short time, palaces, workshops, tombs, roads, cemeteries and thousands of houses also sprang up alongside the temples.

A huge amount of work went into building Akhetaten but after less than twenty years the city was abandoned. After Akhenaten died, the kings of Egypt went back to worshipping many different gods and tried to forget Akhenaten's rule had ever happened. Stone from the city of the sun god was taken to other places like Khemenu (modern El-Ashmunein – it's on the map!) for reuse and everything began to fall into ruin.

It seems like a sad story, but much of Akhetaten survived. It is, in fact, the best-preserved city from ancient Egypt and a sort of time capsule of life 3000 years ago! Today we can discover a huge amount about this ancient place and the lives of the people who lived there. Do you know how we can do this? We do it through Archaeology.

What is Archaeology?

Archaeology is not about searching for hidden treasure but aims to learn about people in the past – people like you and me – by looking at the things they left behind. This might be the ruins of buildings, things that they made and used like pottery, tools or jewellery, and even the food they ate and the bodies of the ancient people themselves. Sometimes these things are buried and we have to slowly and carefully dig them out of the ground; this is called excavation. Everything we find has to be recorded and studied in great detail. Imagine if archaeologists in the future excavated your home as you left it this morning. What might they think about you and your life? It's likely they would get some things wrong! This is why archaeologists have to link together as many different clues as they can to get the story right.

There is archaeology everywhere (any place where people lived in the past). Amarna is an exciting place for archaeologists to work because hundreds of houses have survived alongside the temples and grand tombs. All this evidence is important and gives us information on the lives of people from the very richest to the very poorest. This is why archaeologists from all over the world go there to work and study with Egyptian archaeologists. Archaeologists have been working at Amarna for over 100 years but there is still a lot to learn.

Modern life in the towns around Amarna is equally important. Archaeologists also want to celebrate all the layers of history from the very ancient until today. The modern people of Amarna also have a vital job to do by looking after the ancient city and sharing their stories with visitors. Turn the page to discover what life was like in Amarna for children 3000 years ago and to experience what life is like for children today.

Hello! I'm *Nofret* and this is my twin brother. His name is *Rahotep*. We live in the King's huge new city of Akhetaten.

We moved here from Thebes, several days' travel by boat from the south. Other families came from Memphis in the north or from other smaller towns.

We came following the King, Akhenaten, who wanted to create a new home for the sun god Aten.

When people first arrived here they built their houses close to their family and friends. Everyone tries to help each other out by sharing food, making mudbricks for their houses and collecting water from wells or the river.

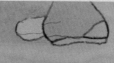

Amarna
Life Under
the Sun

11

Akhenaten brought everyone here because the Aten told him to come.

The land is special because it is the home of the sun god who shines down from above and provides everything we need.

We are near the river Nile, which floods every year and is the giver of life.

We take water from the river using a shaduf, a kind of hoist – it's a fairly new invention!

We use the water to irrigate the rich farmland where we grow crops and animal feed. Much of our food comes from the west bank of the river where the fields stretch as far as the eye can see!

We make mudbricks from the Nile mud and get stone from the royal quarries in the cliffs nearby. The cliffs are also the perfect place to make tombs for the royal family and the King's friends.

Amarna
Life Under the Sun

Our towns are special because they are close to the river Nile.

We like to meet our friends and play by the river as it is so beautiful. The Nile is also really important for crops and animals, as well as fish.

The river doesn't flood anymore. Grandad says this is because a huge dam controls the water in Aswan in the south of Egypt.

Instead, we have lots of special ways of lifting water from the Nile. There are canals which take water to fields far away from the river and mechanical pumps to get the water where we need it most.

A Growing City

Akhenaten's new city has grown very quickly. There are always new buildings appearing!

Dad made our house from mudbrick. He did this with help from other people in our neighbourhood. Some of the inside walls are painted white so that the house looks clean and bright.

Mudbrick helps keep the house cool on hot days and nights. Even the royal palaces are made of mudbrick!

Some of the temples to the sun god were also first built with mudbrick or wood.

Then great white stone buildings took their place.

They shine white in the sunlight and look amazing with all the beautiful pictures, patterns and colourful symbols carved on them by the city's best craftsmen.

The symbols are called hieroglyphs. We can't read them but we know what some of them mean – like a cross within a circle is the hieroglyph for a city!

Life is very exciting in our towns as lots of new building is taking place.

When our grandparents were young, they lived in mudbrick houses. These were built in a similar way to those from the ancient city, with mudbrick walls and the wood and leaves of date palms for the roof.

This meant they were usually only strong enough to reach two floors high.

Today we often still build our own houses but people use modern bricks, cement and metal. This means we can build much taller houses.

The mudbrick houses had thick walls. They stayed quite cool in the summer and warm in the winter, and were often painted white to reflect the sun.

But now lots of us have air conditioning! We like to paint our new houses all sorts of bright colours, like red, yellow, blue and green.

Fashion

We're eight years old and have just got our first proper outfits. Our brothers and sisters are still little and don't always wear clothes.

Our clothes are made from linen. It is very important we keep one outfit clean and white to wear when we celebrate festivals to the Aten or have parties.

When Rahotep is older he'll wear a loin cloth, tunic and kilt and I'll wear a tunic or woman's robe.

Some of our friends wear sandals made from date palm leaves but we like our feet to be free!

We love wearing jewellery. Everyone in the family has at least one amulet. Mum gave them to us to keep us safe.

I wear a bracelet of small beads and little Bes figures, and Rahotep has a new wadjet eye. He broke the last one!

Omar and I like to wear jeans and T-shirts. Omar's T-shirts always make me laugh because he loves ones with really crazy designs!

When we go to help in the fields, we put on our galabeyas. Omar also has a special white galabeya that he wears on Fridays when he goes to visit the mosque with his dad.

My big sister, Fatma, has just turned 11 and has started wearing long skirts and a headscarf.

She and her friends make each other bracelets from colourful thread. She says she'll teach me how to make them.

We wear flipflops most of the time, even when riding our bikes or playing football!

17

Food

We grow loads of delicious food here but every day the best things like beef, ducks and fruit are offered to the sun god at the temples.

Most days we eat bread.

Mum grinds the wheat, mixes it with water and then bakes the bread in our clay oven.

The Nile water can make you sick so we make it into a kind of weak beer. Rahotep doesn't like the beer as it is lumpy and full of bits of barley, but I think it's delicious!

Sometimes we eat fish or have dates and peas. The best days are when Dad brings home a duck or a piece of goat for dinner. That's a real treat as it doesn't happen very often.

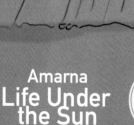

Most families have some farmland close to their home and grow things like onions, carrots, tomatoes, potatoes, aubergines and cucumbers.

We also grow different grasses to feed the animals. I love fresh fruits from our land, like dates and mangos, as they're so sweet.

Wheat is also an important crop. We turn it into flour to make different types of bread like soft *sun bread* with its crispy crust, and thin *bettaw bread* in big sheets ready to be snapped!

Grandma used to grind grain and make bread in a clay oven outside her house. Some people still make their own bread at home in this way but we also buy it from the bakery!

Most days we eat bread with eggs, homemade cheese made from buffalo milk, salad and potatoes, sometimes with fish from the Nile or chicken and rice.

Everyone drinks tea, even children. We also like fizzy drinks! At special events, like weddings, we sometimes have beef, lamb or goat.

Jobs

Dad is a farmer. He works for Ranefer who is the Overseer of the King's horses.

Ranefer owns a lot of land and Dad gets a small portion of the crops.

Rahotep helps Dad in the fields. Sometimes he carries the barley and wheat in baskets to store in the grain silos next to Ranefer's house.

We plant crops in winter once the Nile flood has gone down and harvest just before the sun is at its hottest in summer.

While Rahotep and my little brother are in the fields, I stay home with my five sisters and help Mum in the house.

She is teaching us how to spin thread and weave.

Our community has a new type of loom which allows us to make much wider pieces of cloth, but it's a lot of work! Pleats and loose garments are in fashion – all the royal family wear them.

Life as a Child

When we aren't helping our parents, we like to play in the street or in the courtyard of our house with our cats. The cats bring us good luck and keep away the mice!

One day I'd like to have a pet gazelle like they have in the King's house.

Our mudbrick house has two floors and six rooms, but it is still quite busy when all of us are at home.

We have a hearth, some low stone seats, and stone tables to work on. We have a toy monkey and a rattle that Dad made for us.

Sometimes we like to play games on the roof. We mark out a board and then make gaming pieces from clay!

School takes up most of our day. We get up at 6 o'clock, have breakfast, get dressed and walk to school.

When Grandad was young there was only one school in the town with just 50 children. Now there are lots of schools and thousands more people.

Grandad loves to joke that "You can't see the ground for the children these days!"

After school we have extra lessons to prepare for our exams but by 4 o'clock we go to help on our farm.

We like to eat dinner in front of the TV, watching cartoons.

Omar spends all weekend playing football, basketball and ping-pong. My friends and I like to listen to music, play with our pet cats, watch films and discover new things on the internet!

Getting Around

Our city is really big. We haven't seen most of it as we have to walk everywhere.

One of our neighbours has a bigger house and keeps a donkey.

The royal family don't walk or ride donkeys. They have golden chariots pulled by horses. Twice a day the King, his family and their friends ride along the royal road which runs from the north to the south of the city.

Before they start their journey, the King's foot soldiers clear all the people off the road. Mum says the King stops at the temples for ceremonies and at the palaces to do important business. At the temples, the royal family are joined by musicians, acrobats, dancers and animals to be sacrificed to the sun god. It's an amazing sight and is really noisy.

Everyone knows when the King is coming!

There aren't many cars in our towns. Quite a few people have motorbikes which can weave more easily through the narrow streets.

Some of our friends live far away from their school. This isn't a problem as other people in the neighbourhood help out and give them a lift.

Other children ride a bike to school.

We still have donkeys to help carry things around but not many people ride their donkeys on the larger roads these days.

Dad says the main road between our towns is the same as the royal road that people used in the ancient city. Now we've got cars and tarmac on the road. But Omar and I would both like a chariot!

Tourist buses often go zooming up and down, bringing visitors from all over the world to see the ancient city and the place where we live.

Many of the most important people in Egypt live in our city. The King is number one – he has the power of the Aten and is a god on earth!

The Queen, Nefertiti, is a kind of goddess. She helps the King to keep the universe in order by performing rituals and giving offerings to the sun god.

Tutankhamun, the Prince, will be king one day but he's still too young to help much!

The King and Queen have six daughters. The princesses help their parents to serve the sun god. The royal family have four palaces. The most important officials live in big villas with gardens and ponds.

The Vizier is the second in charge of the country. He does all the administrative jobs that the King does not have time to do. One Vizier lives here but there is another in Memphis.

The High Priest is in charge of the temples for the sun god and the overseers manage important things like the granaries and cattle. Teams of scribes help them with their work.

Amarna
Life Under
the Sun

Today in our communities there are farmers, teachers, doctors, engineers, fishermen, policemen and soldiers.

Most towns used to have an Omda. He was a kind of local chief who helped govern the area.

We still have respected people we go to for advice. We try to make important decisions as a community and we also have a local council.

Our parents have taught us 12 generations of our family names. The names link us to our history and we even know which houses our grandparents and great-grandparents used to live in. We are proud of our long connections to the place we live.

Most days we can see clouds of stone dust at the eastern cliffs where rock is being quarried to make tombs for the King's friends.

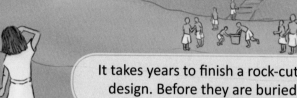

It takes years to finish a rock-cut tomb and each one has a different design. Before they are buried these people will be mummified.

Furniture, linen, food, amulets, a great coffin and all the other things they need for the afterlife will also be collected together.

The burials of our neighbours are much easier as we dig a grave in the desert at the base of the cliffs. We wrap the dead in linen or a mat and place them in their graves with a few offerings for the afterlife, like some jars of beer and pieces of fruit.

Sometime we have feasts to remember the dead and wish them a good life after death. We also hope they will protect us in this life!

Amarna
Life Under the Sun

When a person dies in our town, someone from the family washes the body and wraps it in a special clean white **shroud**.

The body is then taken to the Mosque. The Muslim Imam says prayers for the dead and we have special customs to mourn them for 40 days.

Muslim cemeteries have tombs made of stone or mudbrick with a domed roof, but sometimes bodies are put straight into the ground facing Mecca.

لَا إِلَهَ إِلَّا اللّٰه
مُحَمَّدٌ رَسُولُ اللّٰه

We remember our family members by visiting their graves on the anniversary of their death every year. We take food offerings to give to the poor in honour of the dead.

There are also lots of Christian families in Middle Egypt. Egyptian Christians often have family tombs in their cemeteries which are built in a similar way to our domed tombs.

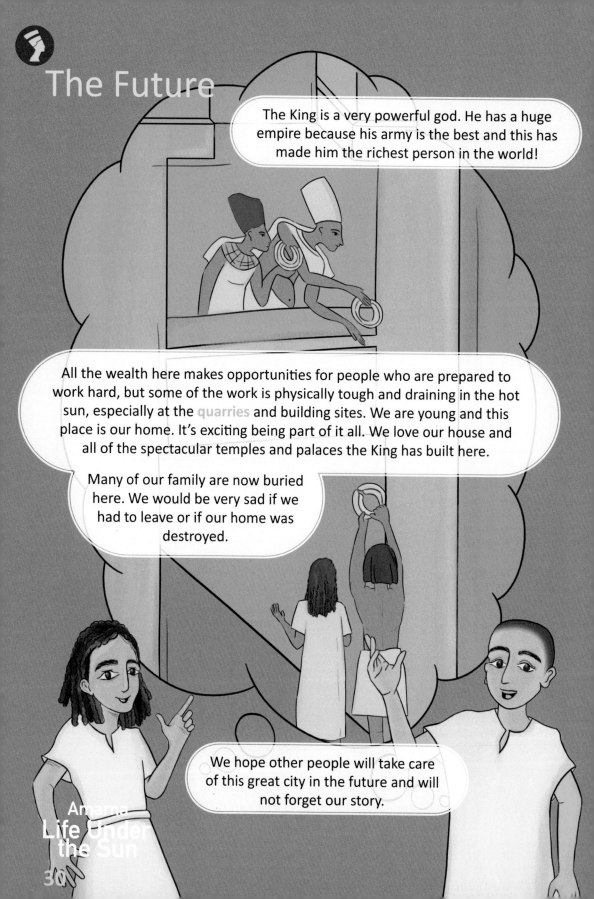

31

Activity 1. Meet the Family

King Amenhotep III – Queen Tiye

King Akhenaten – Queen Nefertiti
(who was known as
Amenhotep IV when he was young)

Akhenaten and Nefertiti's six daughters

**Meritaten | Meketaten | Ankhesenpaaten | Nefernefruaten-tasherit
Neferfeferura | Setepenra**

Akhenaten's son Tutankhamun

The mother of Tutankhamun is
not known. It may have been
Nefertiti or perhaps one of
Akhenaten's other wives (he had
more than one, but Nefertiti was
the most important).

Research Challenge!

Challenge 1.

What can you find out about Nefertiti? Do we know what she looked like? Are there any famous monuments or artefacts (objects) connected to her? Did she live to an old age? Where can you go to see Nefertiti today? Why do you think she is still so famous? Can you find any examples of Nefertiti's image that are used in modern advertising or company logos? What other powerful royal women do you know about from ancient Egypt?

Challenge 2.

Amarna is famous for lots of different reasons, not just people like Nefertiti! The first evidence for an important invention called a 'shaduf' is known from Amarna. Can you find out what a shaduf was? What was it made from? How did it work? Is it similar to anything we use today? Can you find other ancient inventions from Egypt?

Some good places to start researching these questions are museums, libraries and the internet. Maybe you can even ask an archaeologist!

Activity 2. Body Maths

Ancient Egyptian measurements were based on parts of the body. The cubit was the most used unit of measurement. A cubit was based on the distance from an adult's elbow to their fingertips (about 52.5 cm).

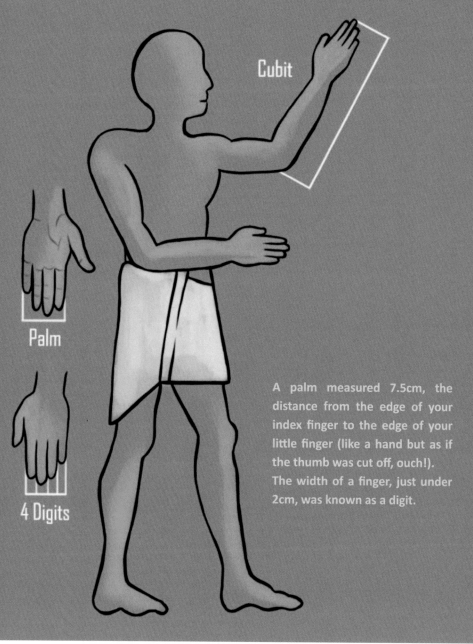

Cubit

Palm

4 Digits

A palm measured 7.5cm, the distance from the edge of your index finger to the edge of your little finger (like a hand but as if the thumb was cut off, ouch!).
The width of a finger, just under 2cm, was known as a digit.

This is an ancient Egyptian cubit rod. It is like a ruler. It is one cubit long (about 52.5 cm) and divided up into 7 palms of 4 digits each, which makes a total of 28 digits. Architects would have used cubit rods when planning large buildings – like the temples at ancient Amarna!

Did you know people still measure things with parts of the body in many countries around the world today? A modern foot is 30cm, about the length of an adult man's foot. This measurement was probably first used by the ancient Greeks!

Measuring Challenge!

Can you measure the things around you using ancient Egyptian measurements?

How tall are you in cubits, palms and digits?

How wide is the room you are in?

What else can you find to measure?

Activity 3. Writing with Lines and Pictures

Most people in ancient Egypt did not know how to read or write. This meant they would have to visit a **scribe** if they wanted to send a letter, which would be written on a thick type of paper made from papyrus reeds. Only the rich could afford to send their children to school to become scribes. **Scribes** did most of the writing in ancient Egypt but other important people like priests and the royal family also learnt how to read and write.

There were two forms of Egyptian writing in use when Amarna was Egypt's capital city. The first was hieroglyphs. Some hieroglyphs look like pictures of the thing they stand for. Can you see how the hieroglyph for an old man looks just like an old man, how the house looks like a drawing of a house and how the hieroglyph for water looks like waves in the water?

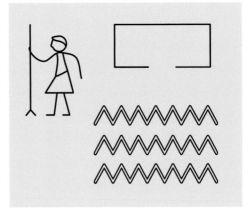

As the written language got more complex, new hieroglyphic symbols were invented. Some of these symbols were linked to a different sound or even a few sounds. Other new symbols had no sounds connected with them at all but were used as visual signs to help explain the full meaning of a word. Hieroglyphs weren't always written one after the other as would seem logical to us today – they were often grouped together. It was a very complicated language!

Hieroglyphs were mainly used in temples and rich people's tombs.

Hieratic was used for more everyday tasks like writing letters and managing the business of the King. Hieratic was based on hieroglyphs but was much faster to write as the shapes were simplified.

Hieroglyphs and hieratic are no longer used in Egypt or anywhere else in the world. In fact, the knowledge of how to read these scripts was forgotten for more than 1000 years! A form of the ancient Egyptian language survived as Coptic, which is still used in the Egyptian Christian church. Coptic is written using the ancient Greek alphabet with a few extra signs. Around 200 years ago, when people became really interested in ancient Egypt, the ancient language had to be cracked like a secret code! The puzzle of the hieroglyphs was finally solved in 1822 by a Frenchman called Jean-François Champollion.

Language Challenge!

Can you decipher these simplified hieroglyphic names using the different letters and sounds shown in the table below? Each group of symbols spells the name of a famous person from Amarna. Each name is written inside a cartouche. A cartouche is an oval shape with a line at one end, which was usually only used to enclose the names of royalty. At Amarna the god Aten had his name written in cartouches too!

Translation tip! English is always written from left to right – *Hello*. Arabic is always written from right to left – مرحبا Hieroglyphs could be written from left to right, right to left, or top to bottom. The only way they could not be written was from bottom to top!

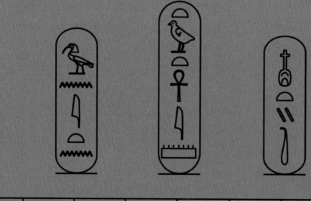

i (or a)	akh	ankh	men	nefer	n	t	ti	u	y

When the cartouches for these three important people were written out in full, they had lots of extra symbols and sometimes parts of the names were moved around. This shows you just how difficult it was to learn to spell in ancient Egypt! Can you figure out which cartouches match the ones you have just deciphered?

Can you spell out your name in simple hieroglyphs?

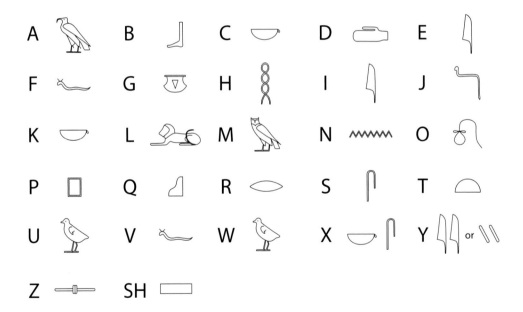

Activity 4. Exploring Protective Powers

Do you have something special you wear or carry around to bring you good luck? In ancient Egypt people of all ages, both rich and poor, would have owned at least one small personal charm or amulet.

An amulet was often worn like a piece of jewellery and could be made in many shapes and colours from different materials like glass, faience, linen, stone and even wood.

The design of each amulet was believed to have different protective powers. Amulets were important to the living but they were also needed to protect the dead.

This is why amulets are often found in mummy wrappings or in graves as they were placed with the bodies of the dead before burial.

Sometimes people were buried with the amulets they wore in life. There were also special amulets that were only used in burials to help the dead in the afterlife.

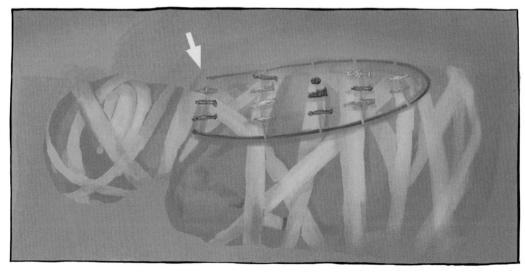

Thousands of amulets with different protective powers have been found during archaeological digs (excavation) at Amarna.

Wadjet eye

Wadjet eye
The most commonly found design for jewellery and amulets at Amarna was the wadjet eye design. Ancient Egyptian stories link the eye to the god Horus who lost his eye in a battle with another god called Seth. The eye probably had protective powers and was worn in life and death. The sign of the eye is also a hieroglyph. When said aloud it would make a word that sounds something like *wadjet*.

Bes
Bes was one of the ancient Egyptian gods. His main job was to protect women and children. Bes was usually shown as a man with dwarfism wearing a scary mask. Sometimes he had a lion's mane and tail and held a tambourine! Lots of small amulets and jewellery pieces in the shape of Bes have been found in the houses at Amarna. These would have been worn especially by the women and children who once lived there to help keep them safe.

Bes

Scarab
Scarab beetle amulets were very common in ancient Egypt. They were linked to the god Khepri who was often shown with the body of a man and the head of a beetle. The flat bottom of scarab amulets was normally decorated with images or hieroglyphs. Scarabs were also linked to rebirth and are often found in burials.

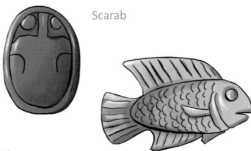

Scarab

Fish
Lots of fish amulets have been found at Amarna. The fish was another symbol of rebirth and was used in burials. Fish amulets were also believed to give protection during life, particularly to children!

Design Challenge!
Now you are an amulet expert! Have a go at designing your own special amulet. What would it look like? Is it based on the shape of an animal, a plant, a person or something totally different? What colour will your amulet be? What protective powers will your amulet have? Why did you choose this shape for your amulet?

Activity 5. Travelling the Royal Road

The royal road was not an ordinary road. It ran through the heart of Akhetaten, from north to south, and was lined with the city's most important buildings. Workers on foot or on donkeys, as well as officials in chariots pulled by horses, used the road. But the most important journeys that took place each day were those made by the King and his entourage.

Twice a day Akhenaten raced along the royal road in his golden chariot. The rest of the royal family joined him for this journey as did his royal bodyguards!

The King was believed to be a living god on earth. He represented the sun god Aten. The King and the Aten were linked together by the royal road. As the King travelled north to south along the road under the sun's shining rays, the Aten (the sun) moved east to west in the sky. On the way, Akhenaten would stop to worship in the city's temples and perhaps take care of important business.

Inside the temples the King was met by his high officials, dancers and musicians. Cattle were brought in to be offered to the sun god. The sights, sounds and smells of all the different people and activities taking place within the temple grounds would have been quite amazing!

You can still walk on a section of the original royal road today! It has survived best where it passes through the temples and palaces of the ruined Central City.

Imagination Challenge!

Imagine you are a worker in one of the temples when the King's procession arrives on the royal road. Write a postcard to a friend explaining what it is like. What's your role during the King's visit? Are you a priest, a dancer, a musician or maybe the person in charge of the animals being offered to the sun god? What can you see? What can you smell? What can you hear? How do you feel? What do you think about the King and the royal family? Draw a picture on the front of the postcard to illustrate your description.

Activity 6. Producing Patterns

The style of art in ancient Amarna was very special. The use of softer, rounder shapes and attention to detail made images seem more alive than in earlier times. Akhenaten and his family embrace each other, like in a family photo. Marching soldiers, whirling dancers and people on speeding chariots look as if they might pop out of the painted scenes at any moment! Plants and trees seem to sway in the breeze. Birds look ready to flap their wings, horses appear ready to gallop and calves leap through the river rushes.

Plants, birds and animals were very important to the ancient Egyptians. They showed the life-giving power of the sun god – the Aten. Artists used the shapes, patterns and colours they saw in nature in the decoration of temples, tombs and houses.

The ancient Egyptians liked to use bright colours. Red, blue, yellow, green and white were the main colours used at ancient Amarna. The walls, ceilings and sometimes even the floors of important houses (especially the royal palaces) were decorated with white daisies, lotus and papyrus plants in scenes of river life or eye-catching patterns.

Stone columns at Amarna were often shaped like plants and the tops were painted to look like date palm leaves or papyrus flowers. Bunches of grapes were sometimes added to designs, as well as waterbirds, butterflies, fish and wild flowers.

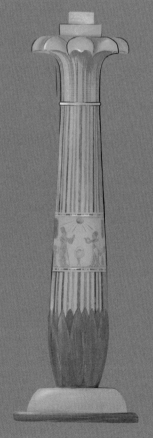

Flowers, fruit, petals and other plants also inspired the design of necklaces and clay pots. These were made in workshops both near the centre of the ancient city and on the outskirts of the housing areas. In some workshops, artists carved statues from stone, in others they made jewellery from precious metals or transformed lumps of clay into beautiful pots.

People also made small items such as jewellery and tools in their own homes. You had to be very self-sufficient in ancient Egypt - if something was needed, you often had to make it yourself!

Art Challenge!

A pattern is made up of a repeated design of colours and shapes. Lots of the patterns created by the artists and craftsmen at Amarna were symmetrical or had repeating motifs. What patterns do you see around you in daily life? What plants, animals, shapes and colours do you like best? Why not combine your favourite things from nature to make your own special repeating pattern inspired by the designs from ancient Amarna? You could turn your pattern into a decoration for a pot or a painting for your house!

Activity 7. Baking Bread and Brewing Beer

For many ancient Egyptians, life was focused on farming. Cereal crops like wheat and barley were needed to make the most important food and drink - bread and very weak beer! Everyone in ancient Amarna from the King to the poorest families would have had these two items with their meals.

Bread and beer were important **offerings** to the gods at temples. At ancient Amarna, there were huge bakeries next to the Great Aten Temple which produced bread for the sun god. Loaves of bread and jars of beer were also needed for the afterlife. Sometimes they were put inside tombs, or scenes of baking bread and **brewing** beer were painted on tomb walls.

Bread is still one of the most widely eaten foods around the world. The main ingredient is normally wheat. There are several kinds of wheat. Today, one type is used to make bread and a different variety is used to make pasta. The ancient Egyptians used another sort of wheat, called emmer wheat, which is hardly grown today. This type has a tough casing around the edible grain that takes a lot of hard work to remove. The ancient Egyptians did this by pounding the grain with a special wooden tool in a large stone bowl to break up the casing, then separating out the grains. After that, they ground the grains of wheat with large stones to make flour.

Once the flour is ready, water then has to be added to create dough. Lots of other ingredients can also be added for flavour, like seeds and oil. Most ancient and modern Egyptian bread is a type of flat bread. This is because it is made without yeast. Yeast is a special kind of edible fungus that makes bread rise and gives it a special taste. Yeast was added to some ancient Egyptian bread, but was not often used.

Bread has to be baked before it is eaten. In ancient Egypt, bread was sometimes cooked over an open fire or on slabs of stone placed over the flames. In ancient Amarna many houses had dome-shaped ovens. The ovens were made from fired clay. They didn't have electricity in ancient Egypt: to heat their ovens they had to build a fire inside. Once the oven wall was really hot the remains of the fire would be carefully removed. Next, the inside of the oven would be quickly wiped with a damp brush or cloth to get rid of the soot.

While one person was doing this job, someone else would be making lots of balls of dough. The balls were then slightly flattened. The bottom of the dough was rubbed with water or milk and stuck onto the hot inner wall of the oven. The leftover heat from the fire would make the bread cook. The bread was ready once it began to lift away from the sides of the oven and the special aroma started to fill the air!

Cookery Challenge!

Why not try making your own ancient Egyptian yeasted bread. Make sure you ask an adult to help you! This recipe makes enough for four small, fist-sized loaves or one big one.

Mix together in a large bowl:
- 250g plain flour
- 180ml of warm water
- Pinch of salt
- 5g yeast (5g is normally the amount in one small packet. The ancient Egyptians did not have sachets of yeast. They probably saved some dough with yeast each time they made yeasted bread, so the next mixture would rise. Because yeast is alive it can grow and multiply in the new dough).

You will also need:
- Small cotton cloth (clingfilm will also work but they didn't have this in ancient Egypt!)

Knead the mixture in the bowl for at least 5 minutes, stretching it out and pressing it down again with your hands. If it seems very wet, add a little more flour. If it seems too dry, add a splash more water.

Cover the bowl with a small cotton cloth and leave the mixture to rise somewhere a little bit warm (not in the fridge!) for 1-2 hours until it has doubled in size. The surface might also have cracked a little.

Knead the dough again and shape it. You might want to split it up into lots of smaller loaves, or make one big one. Ancient Egyptian bread was often round or triangular. Sometimes it was even shaped like a fish or animal. You could try this and see how it comes out! Lay out your shapes on a greased baking sheet and let them sit for another hour to rise again.

Now your bread is ready for the oven. Don't worry if you don't have a clay oven. An electric or gas oven will work too! Make sure the oven is good and hot (220C/400F degrees is about the right temperature). Depending on the size of your loaf, it will take a different amount of time to cook (about 10 minutes for the small loaves and 30 minutes for a large one). You'll know it is ready once it has risen, turned a golden-brown colour and is no longer squashy to touch. Get an adult to help you check your bread is ready so you don't burn yourself!

We don't know exactly what people would have eaten with their bread – perhaps nothing if they were very poor or wanted a quick meal! For a main meal, they might have eaten vegetables like onions, spinach, carrots or lentils with their bread, or fish from the Nile. If they were wealthier, they might have had meat from goats or cattle.

Activity 8. Building with Mud and Stone

Soil (mud) has been used to build things for thousands of years. Soil is almost everywhere. This means it is easy to find. When mixed with water and other materials it can be used in lots of ways. The big problem with buildings made from mud is that they can be easily damaged and need regular repair.

Most buildings in ancient Amarna were made from mudbrick. Only the most important parts of the city – like the temples – were made of stone. The stone was cut into small blocks called talatat at the nearby quarries. The blocks were designed to be carried by one strong person. Look back at the measuring challenge to figure out how big a talatat block was. It measured one cubit long by half a cubit wide and half a cubit thick. Do you think you would be strong enough to carry one?

Mudbricks were used to build all the houses in ancient Amarna, even the house of the King! Mudbricks were much thinner and lighter than stone blocks and varied in size depending on how they were made. In ancient Amarna, mudbricks measured about 34cm long, 17cm wide and 8cm thick.

Soil from near the river Nile made the best mudbricks. The mud was mixed with sand and gravel from the desert and water was added to help hold it together. The wet mudbrick mix was then put into a rectangular wooden mould to give it the right shape. The mould was then lifted off the brick which was left in the sun to dry.

To build a wall, the bricks were laid out in overlapping patterns. This helped to make the wall stronger. The bricks were fixed in place with a wet layer of mud called mortar. When the mud dried it held the bricks firmly together.

Once a wall was finished, it would be plastered inside and out. The plaster was also made of mud. The mud was turned into a paste with water, and bits of straw were added to stop the plaster cracking when it dried. Some of the mudbrick houses at ancient Amarna were painted white inside. In the larger houses belonging to important people in the city, beautiful coloured paintings were sometimes placed on the walls, ceilings and around the doorways, as you saw in the Producing Patterns activity.

Windows and doors were made of wood or stone and often painted red. Floors could be made of mud plaster or brick, but were often just the natural ground smoothed flat by water and the trampling of feet.

Roofs were flat and were usually supported by wooden beams held up by columns in the larger rooms. The beams would be covered in mats or plant material and a layer of mud. If the roof was strong enough, the house might have a second storey.

Mudbrick is a good insulator. This means it helps keep houses cool in summer and warm in winter. As there was no heating or air conditioning in ancient Egypt, this would have been really important!

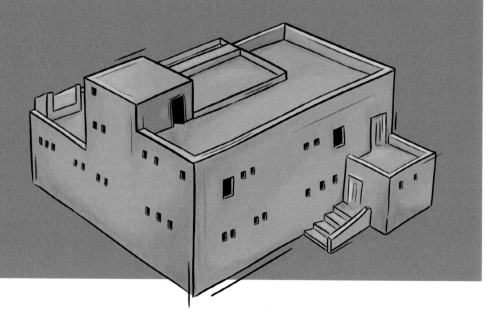

Science Challenge!

Can you follow the ancient Egyptian method below to make your own mudbricks? Perhaps you can try adding different amounts of sand, gravel or straw to your mud mix to see what makes the strongest brick? You can test the strength by placing the ends of your brick across a gap between two strong boxes. Gradually add small weights to the middle of the brick and see how many it can take before it breaks. Make sure your toes are not in the way when the brick cracks!

You will need:

- a small but strong plastic box you can pierce holes into that will act as your brick mould. The ancient Egyptians didn't have plastic as it wasn't invented. Their brick moulds were made of wood. For our experiment, plastic butter tubs are ideal but something a bit bigger or smaller will also work!
- plenty of soil (mud) (get an adult with gardening gloves to check there are no sharp objects in the mud)
- water
- sharp scissors (get an adult to help you)
- a good supply of sand and/or gravel (small stones) – you could also use some chopped up straw if you have it
- a large container like a plastic bucket or dustbin

Step 1. Prepare the soil by crumbling up any big lumps and removing large stones or pieces of twig.

Step 2. Use a stick to mix the soil and water together in your large container to create a thick mud (it should be just wet enough to stick together - a bit like the bread dough!).

Step 3. Add a few handfuls of sand, gravel and/or straw (we call these additions *temper*) to stop your bricks from cracking.

Step 4. Mix the mud and temper together really thoroughly.

Step 5. Use the scissors to pierce a few large holes in the bottom of your small plastic container so the air can get in (this will stop your mud mix from getting stuck). Get an adult to help with the scissors and watch your fingers! Then scoop in the mixture. Make sure you fill the brick moulds to the top and pat them down firmly. This will help to make the surface flat and remove any air bubbles.

Step 6. Turn your brick out straight away by quickly but carefully flipping the mould upside-down onto a wooden board or surface covered with sand or straw (so it doesn't stick!). Then gently lift off the plastic container ready to use for your next brick. If your brick starts to sag or slump the mixture is too wet. Try adding some more soil. If your brick crumbles and starts to fall apart your mixture is too dry. Try adding a little more water.

Step 7. Let the bricks dry in the sun (you need to be patient – this could take a few days or even weeks!). You'll know the bricks are dry when their colour has changed to a lighter shade of brown or grey all over and they feel totally dry to touch.

After the bricks have dried, they are ready to be used in your strength experiments. What are your conclusions? What is the best temper or mix of tempers? What is the ideal amount of temper to add to make the strongest bricks? How much weight can your different bricks hold? Would you trust your bricks to build a wall?

Activity 9. Creating Fabric and Fashion

Just like today, clothes and other textiles (fabrics) were important in all areas of ancient Egyptian life. At Amarna we can tell a lot about the things people wore by looking at scenes from tombs and temples. Archaeologists also find the remains of many different textile items when they excavate houses and graves.

Linen, which is made from a plant called flax, was the most widely used cloth in ancient Egypt. Sheep's wool, goat hair and fibres from the bark of palm trees were also used to make fabric.

Thread or yarn was made from plant or animal fibres by spinning. This involved twisting lots of the thin fibres together to make longer and thicker strands. The thread was then wound into balls. The thread was sometimes bleached to make it white by washing it and drying it in the sun. It could also be coloured using dyes made from plants and other natural materials, but most clothes were made from undyed and unbleached thread. Once the thread was ready, it could be woven into cloth on a loom.

A loom is a large weaving tool. Long threads are fixed between either end of the loom. Thread is then passed under and over these fixed strands to create an interlocking mesh called a weave.

Today we use machines to weave cloth, but in ancient Egypt this was done by hand. There were two main types of loom in ancient Amarna. One could be used in an upright position fixed into blocks set into the floor or leant against a wall. Another ran along the floor and was fixed into wooden beams raised just off the ground. The upright loom was popular in ancient Amarna because it was good for making larger pieces of fabric. This created a new fashion for pleats and folds in the clothes of the rich.

Technology Challenge!

In ancient Amarna, fabric was made in workshops as well as in people's homes. Kilts were popular with wealthy men, while women from rich families often wrapped themselves in a large piece of cloth that was held in place by a knot or belt. Sometimes the clothes of the wealthy were pleated and fringed, or even dyed or woven in bright colours.

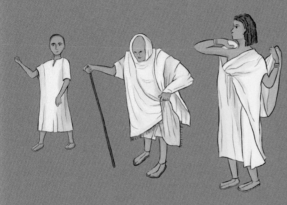

Men and women from poorer families in ancient Amarna would all have worn simple bag-tunics. These were made from large rectangular pieces of cloth, folded over and stitched up the sides. A slit or keyhole-shape would be cut in the top for the head. When working in the fields, men would have worn loin-cloths (a sort of triangular-shaped underwear). Young children often would have gone about unclothed in the warmer months! When they reached about eight years old, they started wearing the same style clothes as their parents.

Many people in ancient Amarna were very poor and probably didn't wear anything on their feet! Those who could afford it wore sandals made from leather, date palm leaves and grasses.

Why not have a go at weaving your own cloth?

What you'll need:
- 1 small piece of hard cardboard (like from a cardboard box, 12cm x 12cm square is a good size but you can go bigger!)
- pen or pencil
- scissors
- 1 small ball of wool or thread, or several long lengths of different coloured wool or thread
- ruler
- sticky tape
- tapestry needles (these aren't essential as explained below)

Step 1. Use your ruler to draw a border at the edge of your card, around 2cm in from each side of your loom.

Step 2. On two opposite sides, draw lines for the notches. These should be around 0.5cm apart and reach all the way across the loom from between your 2cm marks and the edge of your card.

Step 3. Carefully cut along the lines you've drawn for the notches, stopping at the border line.

Step 4. Tape the end of one strong thread to the back of the loom (the unmarked side). Pass the thread through the first notch at the top left of the card and wrap it over the front of the loom and through the opposite notch at the bottom of the card. Continue doing this all the way across the loom (like in the picture on the next page) and tape it to the back.

Step 5. Cut a new length of thread (around 2 cubits long). You can either attach the

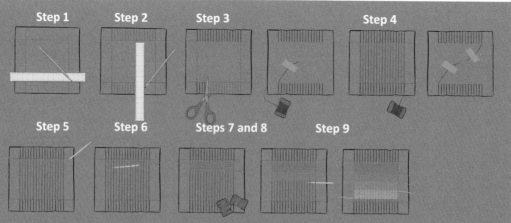

Step 1   Step 2   Step 3   Step 4

Step 5   Step 6   Steps 7 and 8   Step 9

thread to a tapestry needle (and make a knot so it doesn't fall out), or wrap a small piece of tape around the end of the thread – making it more solid – and weave with it directly.

Step 6. Guide the thread through the loom in an under-over pattern. Go under the first string, over the second, under the next and so on until you reach the other side of the loom. Pull the thread through leaving around 5cm sticking out the end. Push the thread up to the top of the loom towards the notches.

Step 7. Bring the thread back through the loom from the side you just exited. This time you need to use the opposite pattern compared with your first line. This means you need to start the second line by going over the top of the first string if you just went under it, or by going under it if you just went over it. Continue the under-over or over-under pattern until you reach the other side. Pull the thread through but not too tight so it doesn't bend the string of the loom! Push the second line of thread up to meet the first.

Step 8. Keep adding new rows by alternating the over-under pattern and don't forget to push the thread up so that each thread touches.

Step 9. If your thread runs out or you want to add a new colour, you can add a new thread. Leave a tail on the side of the loom where the thread finishes. On the same side, add the new colour just like you did in Step 6. Make sure you're continuing the

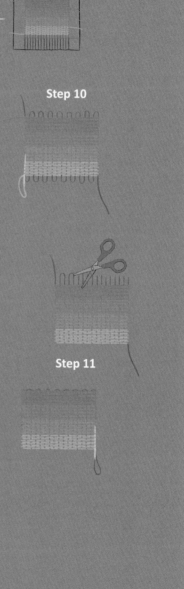

Step 10

Step 11

54

correct under-over or over-under pattern and carry on weaving.

Step 10. Once you've filled up your loom, you can tidy up the loose ends by threading them back inside the weaving a couple of centimetres down the side of the support threads. Then pass the thread back to the outside, gently pull it tight and cut off the rest of the tail.

Step 11. To finish your weaving, remove the tape from your original thread on the back of the loom and unhook it from the notches.

Push the weaving down onto the bottom loops as far as it will go. Now you have longer top loops. Cut these in the middle and tie the two ends together neatly. Finally, tie the two long ends that were taped to the back of the loom neatly to the nearest under-over, over-under woven thread and tuck the end inside of your weaving like in Step 10.

You're done! What might you do with your finished product?

Activity 10. Visiting Amarna

Egypt is a very popular tourist destination. Millions of people travel from all over the world to visit the country each year. Most tourists do not go to Amarna. This means they miss out on discovering the amazing history of the site and meeting its modern people.

Tourist Challenge!

Can you come up with an idea to attract tourists to visit Amarna? Perhaps you can design a tourist information poster or leaflet showing what is special about Amarna. Maybe you can think of a catchy slogan to get people's attention. You might want to include a map to show people where Amarna is in Egypt. To help visitors take care of Amarna on their visit, you could also add some tips on good behaviour at archaeological sites. You might include things like 'please don't drop litter or walk on the ruins'. Can you think of any more top tips to protect the site?

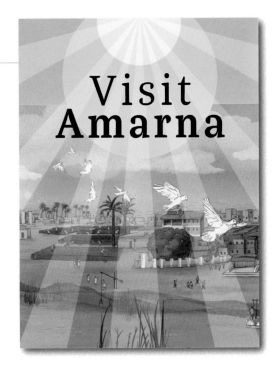

Glossary

Abandoned – when something is left behind or given up on

Amulet – a small object, like a piece of jewellery, believed to have protective or magic powers

Architects – people who plan and design buildings

Banned – when something is officially stopped or forbidden

Brewing – the activity of making beer

Dam – a barrier built across a river to hold back water

Dough – a thick mixture of flour and water that is baked into bread

Dwarfism – a condition that causes a person to be unusually short

Entourage – a group of people around and looking after the needs of an important person

Evidence – something information can be obtained from, like an ancient object, building or inscription

Faience – a brightly coloured and shiny glazed material (a bit like glass), which is often blue

Fungus – a plant with no flowers or green leaves, like a mushroom or mould

Galabeya – a traditional item of Egyptian clothing, like a long robe

Generation – a period of about 30 years that separates people of different ages, e.g. a baby, mother and grandmother are from 3 different generations of one family

Granaries – places where grain is stored

Hearth – a fireplace

Imam – the person who leads prayers in a mosque (an Islamic holy building)

Irrigate – to channel water to plants to help them grow

Kilt – an item of clothing a bit like a knee-length skirt

Linen – cloth made from the fibres of the flax plant

Loin cloth – a small piece of cloth worn like underwear

Loom – a frame used for weaving fabrics

Mecca – located in Saudi Arabia, it is the holiest city in Islam

Motifs – artistic designs often creating patterns

Offerings – things that are given to someone, a bit like gifts, e.g. food left for a god as part of a religious practice

Overseers – people who supervise others, especially workers

Papyrus – a material similar to thick paper, which is made from the stem of a papyrus plant

Pleats – decorative folds in an item of clothing

Quarries – places where stone is dug or cut out from the ground

Recorded – when something is written down, drawn or photographed

Rebirth – being born again, for example, after death into an afterlife

Rituals – special religious or ceremonial actions

Scribe – a person whose job is to write and copy documents

Self-sufficient – when a person is able to produce everything they need

Shroud – a piece of cloth in which a dead person is wrapped for burial

Silos – round buildings used to store grain within granaries

Soot – a black powder that is left by smoke from a fire

Symmetrical – when one half of a design is reflected on the other side, like a mirror image

Tambourine – a musical instrument, like a small drum with metal discs around the sides, which you shake or hit with your hand

Time capsule – a container holding items from one particular time period

Tunic – a sleeveless item of clothing worn on the upper body, a bit like a long t-shirt or dress

Vizier – the King's highest-ranking political advisor, like a Prime Minister

المحتويات

مرحبا بكم في تل العمارنة!

مصر بلد لديه العديد من القصص الرائعة ليحكيها. فمنذ التاريخ القديم وحتى اليوم، مازالت الناس، والأماكن، والمباني، والتقاليد تستحوذ على خيال العالم. ويستكشف هذا الكتاب أحد الأماكن الخاصة في مصر – تل العمارنة. لقد كانت تل العمارنة مدينة عظيمة في التاريخ القديم، أما اليوم فهي موطن لمجتمع حديث يعيش بجانب (وأحيانا فوق) الأطلال القديمة.

واليوم، يسكن تل العمارنة ما يزيد عن 25000 نسمة في قرى تل بني عمران (التل)، والحاج قنديل، والعمارية. وإذا نظرتم بعناية، ستجدون بين المنازل الحديثة، والمدارس، والطرق، والأراضي الزراعية أدلة تشير إلى الوقت الذي كانت فيه تل العمارنة أهم مدينة في مصر كلها!

تقع تل العمارنة في منتصف المسافة بين القاهرة في الشمال والأقصر في الجنوب. انظروا إن كان باستطاعتكم أن تجدوا القاهرة، وتل العمارنة، والأقصر على الخريطة! وتقع تل العمارنة على الضفة الشرقية لنهر النيل العظيم.

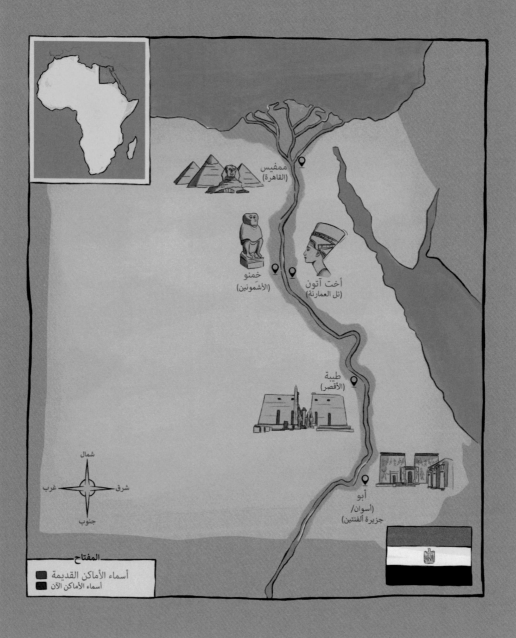

فمنذ أكثر من 3000 سنة كان لتل العمارنة اسم مختلف. لقد كانت تُدعى أخت آتون. هكذا تُكتَب أخت آتون بالهيروغليفية – لغة الكتابة عند قدماء المصريين.

هل ترون الرمز الأول على اليسار والذي يشبه طلوع الشمس من بين جبلين؟ إن كلمة أخت آتون تعني "أفق قرص الشمس" في اللغة المصرية القديمة: وعلامة الجبلين هي الأفق (أخت) والعلامات الموجودة على اليمين تُقرأ آتون (الشمس).

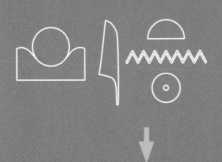

لقد أمر الفرعون إخناتون ببناء هذه المدينة. وفي أخت آتون بدأ في عبادة أول دين معروف يركز على إله واحد فقط، إله الشمس، سماه آتون. وقام بحظر عبادة الآلهة الأخرى في مصر القديمة! ولإرضاء الملك، أتى الناس من جميع أنحاء مصرليساعدوا في بناء عاصمته الجديدة من الطوب اللبن والحجارة. كما انتقلت زوجة إخناتون، نفرتيتي، وعائلته إلى العاصمة الجديدة لدعم الملك. وقد ركزت الحياة في المدينة على عبادة إله الشمس. وكانت هناك حاجة إلى النحاتين، والكتّاب، والبنائين، والمزارعين، والإداريين، والحرفيين.

انظروا صفحة المسرد، صفحة 56، لمعرفة معاني الكلمات المكتوبة باللون البرتقالي!

وفي قلب الدينة، كانت هناك معابد كبيرة في الهواء الطلق فيها تماثيل بديعة. لقد كانت أماكن مزدحمة، حيث كان الكثير من الوقت يمضي في إعداد القرابين لإله الشمس. وفي وقت قصير، ظهرت القصور، والورش، والطرق، والجبانات، والآلاف من المنازل بجانب المعابد.

لقد أخذ بناء أخت آتون قدرا هائلا من العمل، ولكن بعد أقل من عشرين عاما أصبحت المدينة مهجورة. فبعد وفاة إخناتون، عاد ملوك مصر إلى عبادة العديد من الآلهة المختلفة وحاولوا نسيان فترة حكم إخناتون. وقد تم نقل الحجارة من مدينة إله الشمس إلى أماكن أخرى مثل خمنو (قرية الأشمونين حاليا) من أجل إعادة استخدامها، وبدأ كل شيء في الانهيار.

إنها تبدو كقصة حزينة، ولكن الكثير من أخت آتون تحدّى الزمن وعاش. إنها، في الحقيقة، أكثر المدن حفظا التي وصلتنا من مصر القديمة وكأنها كبسولة زمنية حفظت الحياة من ثلاثة ألاف سنة. واليوم، يمكننا معرفة الكثير عن هذه الأماكن القديمة وعن حياة الناس الذين عاشوا هناك. هل تعرفون كيف يمكننا فعل ذلك؟ يمكننا أن نفعل ذلك من خلال علم الآثار.

ما هو علم الآثار؟

إن علم الآثار لا يتعلق بالبحث عن الكنوز المخفية ولكنه يهدف إلى معرفة الأشخاص الذين عاشوا في الماضي – أشخاص مثلي ومثلك – من خلال النظر إلى الأشياء التي تركوها وراءهم. وقد تكون هذه الأشياء أطلال مبان، أو أشياء صنعوها واستعملوها مثل الفخار، أو أدوات، أو مجوهرات، وحتى الطعام الذي كانوا يأكلونه وأجساد القدماء أنفسهم. وأحيانا ما تكون هذه الأشياء مدفونة في الأرض ولابد أن نحفر ببطء وعناية لإخراجها من باطن الأرض؛ وهذا ما يسمى التنقيب. فكل ما نجده يجب تسجيله ودراسته بأدق التفاصيل. تخيل إذا ما قام علماء الآثار، في المستقبل، بالحفر في منزلك كما تركته هذا الصباح، فما الذي سيفكرون فيه بالنسبة لك ولحياتك. من المحتمل أنهم سيستنتجون بعض النتائج الخاطئة! ولهذا السبب فإن علماء الآثار يجب أن يربطوا معا العديد من القرائن المختلفة قدر الإمكان لجعل القصة صحيحة.

إن علم الآثار في كل مكان (في أي مكان عاش فيه الناس في الماضي). وتعتبر تل العمارنة مكانا مثيرا لعمل علماء الآثار لأن المئات من المنازل قد نجت إلى جانب المعابد والمقابر الكبيرة. وكل هذه الأدلة مهمة وتمدنا بالمعلومات عن حياة الناس من أفقرهم إلى أغناهم. ولهذا يأتي علماء الآثار من كل أنحاء العالم للعمل والدراسة مع علماء الآثار المصريين. إن علماء الآثار يعملون في تل العمارنة منذ مئة سنة، ولايزال هناك الكثير لتعلمه.

وتحظى الحياة الحديثة في القرى المحيطة بتل العمارنة بنفس القدر من الأهمية. فعلماء الآثار يولون الاهتمام بكل العصور التاريخية من أقدمها وحتى أحدثها. وللأشخاص الذين يعيشون اليوم في تل العمارنة وظيفة مهمة من خلال العناية بالمدينة القديمة ومشاركة قصصهم مع زوارها. اقلبوا الصفحة لتتعرفوا على كيف كانت الحياة في تل العمارنة بالنسبة للأطفال منذ 3000 سنة وما هو شكل الحياة بالنسبة لأطفال اليوم.

مرحبا! اسمي نوفرت، وهذا هو أخي التوأم. اسمه راحوتب. نحن نسكن في أخت آتون، المدينة الملكية الكبيرة.

لقد انتقلنا إلى هنا من طيبة في الجنوب، عن طريق السفر بالمركب لعدة أيام. وهناك عائلات أخرى جاءت من ممفيس في الشمال أو من مدن أخرى أصغر.

وقد جئنا إلى هنا، بعد أن أتى الملك إخناتون الذي أراد إنشاء بيت جديد لإله الشمس آتون.

وفي البداية، عندما وصل الناس إلى هنا، قاموا ببناء بيوتهم بالقرب من عائلاتهم وأصدقائهم. وحاول الجميع مساعدة بعضهم البعض من خلال المشاركة في الطعام، وصنع الطوب اللبن لمنازلهم، وجمع المياه من الآبار أو النهر.

مرحبا! اسمي أميرة، وهذا عمر ابن عمي. أنا أسكن في قرية التل وعمر يسكن بالقرب مني في قرية الحاج قنديل. إن قريتينا عبارة عن عائلات كبيرة ونحن نساعد بعضنا البعض حين نستطيع.

ويقول جدي إن ذلك يعود إلى أن الكثير من العائلات يعيشون هنا منذ أجيال، ربما منذ أكثر من 150 سنة.

وقد عمل بعض أفراد أسرتنا مع أول بعثة حفريات في تل العمارنة، مع عالم الآثار البريطاني فليندرز بيتري في تسعينيات القرن التاسع عشر. وكان هوارد كارتر عضوا في فريق بيتري. إنه الرجل الذي اكتشف مقبرة توت عنخ آمون في وادي الملوك سنة 1922.

Amarna
Life Under the Sun

هل تعرفون أن توت عنخ آمون قد عاش في تل العمارنة عندما كان صبيا؟

لقد قام إخناتون بإحضار الجميع إلى هنا لأن آتون قال له ذلك.

فالأرض مميزة لأنها موطن إله الشمس الذي يضيء من فوق ويوفر كل ما نحتاجه.

كما أننا بالقرب من نهر النيل ، الذي يفيض كل عام وهو واهب الحياة.

كما أننا نأخذ الماء من النهر باستخدام الشادوف، وهو اختراع جديد إلى حد ما.

نحن نستخدم المياه لري الأراضي الزراعية الغنية لزراعة المحاصيل وأعلاف الحيوانات.
ويأتي معظم غذائنا من الضفة الغربية للنهر حيث تمتد الحقول إلى أقصى ما تستطيع العين رؤيته!

كما نصنع الطوب اللبن من طمي النيل ونحصل على الأحجار من المحاجر الملكية التي تقع على المنحدرات القريبة. والمنحدرات، أيضا، هي مكان مثالي لبناء مقابر العائلة الملكية وأصدقاء الملك.

إن قرانا مميزة لأنها بالقرب من نهر النيل.

ونحن نحب أن نلتقي بأصدقائنا وأن نلعب بجانب النهر لأنه جميل جدا. والنيل مهم جدا للمحاصيل، والحيوانات، والأسماك.

لقد توقف فيضان النيل الآن. يقول جدي إن سبب ذلك يعود إلى بناء سد ضخم، يتحكم في المياه، في أسوان، جنوب مصر.

والآن لدينا الكثير من الطرق الخاصة لرفع المياه من النيل. فهناك القنوات التي تنقل الماء إلى الحقول البعيدة عن النهر، والمضخات الميكانيكية التي تضخ الماء الذي نحتاج إليه بشدة.

Amarna
Life Under
the Sun

13

مدينة متنامية

لقد تمت مدينة إخناتون الجديدة بسرعة. فهناك دائماً الكثير من المباني التي تظهر!

وقد قام أبي ببناء منزلنا من الطوب اللبن. وقد فعل هذا بمساعدة آخرين يسكنون في حينا. وبعض الجدران الداخلية مطلية باللون الأبيض مما يجعل المنزل نظيفا ومشرقا.

ويساعد الطوب اللبن على بقاء المنزل باردا في الأيام والليالي الحارة. وحتى الأماكن الملكية كانت مبنية من الطوب اللبن!

كما أن بعض المعابد المكرسة لإله الشمس كانت مبنية من الطوب اللبن أو الخشب.

وبعد ذلك حلت المباني الحجرية البيضاء الكبيرة مكانها.

فلونها الأبيض يلمع تحت أشعة الشمس وهي تبدو رائعة بصورها الجميلة والأنماط والرموز الملونة المنحوتة عليها من قبل أفضل الحرفيين في المدينة.

وهذه الرموز تسمى الهيروغليفية. ونحن لا نستطيع قراءتها ولكننا نعرف معاني بعضها – مثل الصليب داخل دائرة والذي يعني في الهيروغليفية كلمة مدينة!

الحياة مثيرة للغاية في قرانا حيث توجد الكثير من المباني.

وعندما كان أجدادنا صغارا، كانوا يسكنون في بيوت من الطوب اللبن. وكانت هذه المنازل مبنية بطريقة مشابهة لمثيلتها في المدينة القديمة، بجدران من الطوب اللبن وسقف من جريد النخيل مما يعني أنها لم تكن تتحمل أكثر من طابقين.

واليوم ما زلنا، في كثير من الأحيان، نبني منازلنا، ولكن الناس يستخدمون الطوب الأحمر والأسمنت والحديد، مما يعني أننا نستطيع بناء بيوت أعلى.

وقديما كانت جدران المنازل المبنية من الطوب اللبن سميكة، ولذلك كانت باردة في الصيف، ودافئة في الشتاء، وغالبا ما كانت تُطلى باللون الأبيض ليعكس أشعة الشمس.

Amarna
Life Under
the Sun

15

ولكن الآن، يملك الكثير منا أجهزة لتكييف الهواء!كما أننا نحب أن نطلي بيوتنا بألوان زاهية مثل الأحمر، والأصفر، والأزرق، والأخضر.

نحن في الثامنة من العمر وقد حصلنا على أول أزيائنا المناسبة. إن إخواننا وأخواتنا مازالوا صغارا ولذلك لا يرتدون ملابس دائما.

إن ملابسنا مصنوعة من الكتان. ومن الأهمية بمكان أن نحتفظ بزي واحد نظيف وأبيض لارتدائه في الاحتفال بأعياد آتون وفي الحفلات.

وعندما يكبر راحوتب سوف يرتدي نقبة، وسترة، وكلت (ملبس شبيه بالتنورة)، أما أنا فسأرتدي سترة أو ثوبا نسائيا.

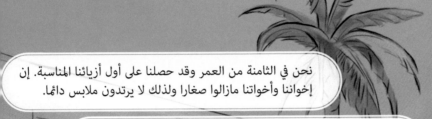

إن البعض من أصحابنا يرتدون صندالا مصنوعة من أوراق النخيل ولكننا نحب أن تكون أقدامنا حرة! نحن أيضا نحب لبس المجوهرات.

وكل فرد في الأسرة لديه، على الأقل، تميمة واحدة. لقد أعطتنا ماما إياها للحفاظ على سلامتنا.

أنا أرتدي سوارا صغيرا من الخرز وأشكال صغيرة من الإله بس، وراحوتب لديه تميمة عليها عين الوجات الزرقاء. لقد كسر التميمة الأخيرة!

أنا وعمر نحب ارتداء البناطيل الجينز والتي شيرتات. وتي شيرت عمر يجعلني اضحك دائما لأنه يحب التي شيرتات ذات التصميمات الغريبة.

ولكن عندما نذهب للعمل في الحقل فإننا نرتدي الجلابية. عمر لديه أيضا جلابية بيضاء خاصة بيوم الجمعة؛ يرتديها عندما يذهب إلى المسجد مع والده.

أختي الكبيرة فاطمة أصبحت في الحادية عشرة من عمرها وبدأت ترتدي الجيبات الطويلة والحجاب. إنها وأصدقائها يصنعون أساور من الخيوط الملونة لبعضهن البعض. لقد وعدتني أن تعلمني كيفية عملها.

نحن نرتدي الشباشب معظم الوقت، حتى ونحن نركب العجل أو نلعب كرة القدم.

نحن نزرع كميات كبيرة من الطعام اللذيذ ولكن، كل يوم، يتم تقديم أفضل الأطعمة مثل اللحوم، والبط والفاكهة كقرابين لإله الشمس في المعابد.

وفي معظم الأيام نأكل الخبز حيث تطحن أمي القمح، وتعجنه بالماء ثم تخبزه في الفرن المصنوع من الطين.

إن مياه النيل قد تجعلك مريضا ولذلك نصنع منها نوعا من الجعة الخفيفة. أخي راحوتب لا يحب الجعة لأنها ثقيلة ومليئة ببقايا الشعير، ولكني أعتقد أنها لذيذة! وفي بعض الأحيان نأكل السمك أو البلح والبسلة.

وأفضل الأيام، عندما يجلب أبي إلى البيت بطة أو قطعة من لحم الماعز للعشاء. هذه متعة حقيقية لأنها لا تحدث في كثير من الأحيان.

معظم الأسر لديها أرض زراعية بالقرب من البيت الذي يسكنون فيه، حيث يزرعون البصل، والجزر، والطماطم، والبطاطس، والباذنجان، والخيار. ونحن نزرع ايضا أنواعا مختلفة من الحشائش لإطعام الحيوانات.

أنا أحب الفواكه الطازجة التي نزرعها في أرضنا مثل البلح والمانجو، لأنها حلوة جدا.

والقمح أيضا محصول مهم. نحن نصنع منه الدقيق لعمل أنواع مختلفة من الخبز مثل العيش الشمسي بقشرته المقرمشة والعيش البتاو. وقد كانت جدتي تطحن الحبوب وتخبز العيش في فرن مصنوع من الطين خارج منزلها!

وإلى اليوم، ما زال بعض الناس يخبزون العيش في البيت بنفس الطريقة ولكننا أيضا نشتريه من المخبز!

وفي معظم الأيام نأكل الخبز مع البيض، أو الجبن البيتي المصنوع من لبن الجاموسة، أو سلطة وبطاطس، وأحيانا ما نأكله مع سمك من النيل أو فراخ وأرز. والجميع يشربون الشاي، حتى الأطفال. كما أننا نحب المياه الغازية!

وفي بعض المناسبات الخاصة، مثل الأفراح، أحيانا ما يكون لدينا لحم البقر، أو الضأن، أو الماعز.

أبي مزارع. وهو يعمل لدى رانفر المشرف على خيول الملك. رانفر يملك الكثير من الأراضي وأبي يحصل على جزء صغير من المحصول.

راحوتب يساعد أبي في الحقل.

وأحيانا يحمل الشعير والقمح في سلال لتخزينها في صوامع الغلال بالقرب من منزل رانفر. نحن نزرع المحاصيل في الشتاء بعد انحسار فيضان النيل ونحصدها قبل اشتداد حرارة الشمس في الصيف.

وبينما يكون راحوتب وأخي الصغير في الحقل، أمكث أنا وأخواتي الخمسة الصغيرات في البيت لمساعدة أمي. إنها تعلمنا كيف نغزل الخيوط وننسجها.

وهناك نوع جديد من الأنوال يسمح لنا بنسج قماش أعرض، ولكنه عمل كثير!

إن الطيات والملابس الفضفاضة هي الموضة الآن – كل أفراد العائلة الملكية يرتدونها.

أباؤنا يعملون معا. وبالإضافة إلى زراعة أرضنا، فإنهم يعملون مع علماء الآثار الذين يأتون من كافة أنحاء العالم للتنقيب في تل العمارنة.

وأحيانا ما يخبرنا أباؤنا عن الأشياء التي وجدوها أثناء عملهم في أراضي الدفن القديمة، والمنازل، والمعابد، مثل قطع الفخار المكسور وعظام الحيوانات.

وأحيانا ما ننسى أنا وعمر أن المدينة القديمة لا تزال حولنا.

وهي تبدو اليوم وكأنها جدران قديمة مهدمة، أو نتوءات ومطبات في الأرض، ولذلك من الصعب أن أتخيل أنها كانت أهم مكان في مصر منذ ثلاثة آلاف سنة!

Amarna
Life Under
the Sun

الحياة كطفل

في الوقت الذي لا نساعد فيه أباءنا، نحب أن نلعب مع القطط في الشارع أو في فناء منزلنا. فالقطط تجلب الحظ وتبعد الفئران عنا!

ويوما ما، أريد أن يكون عندي غزالة كتلك الموجودة في قصر الملك.

يتكون منزلنا، المبني من الطوب اللبن، من طابقين وست غرف، ولكنه يصبح مزدحما عندما نكون جميعا في المنزل.

في منزلنا موقد، وبعض المقاعد الحجرية المنخفضة، وبعض الطاولات الحجرية للعمل عليها.

ولدينا لعبة على شكل قرد وشخشيخة صنعها أبي لنا. وأحيانا ما نحب أن نلعب بعض الألعاب على السطوح. نرسم لوح على الأرض ونصنع قطع اللعبة من الطين!

المدرسة تأخذ معظم وقتنا. نحن نستيقظ في السادسة صباحا، نفطر، ثم نرتدي ملابسنا ونمشي إلى المدرسة.

عندما كان جدي صغيرا لم تكن هناك إلا مدرسة واحدة بها خمسون تلميذا. والآن، هناك الكثير من المدارس والآلاف من الطلاب.

يحب جدي أن يمزح قائلا "هذه الأيام، لا تستطيع أن ترى الأرض من كثرة الأطفال"!

وبعد المدرسة نذاكر للامتحانات، ولكن في الساعة الرابعة نذهب للمساعدة في الحقل.

نحن نحب أن نأكل العشاء أمام التليفزيون، ونحن نشاهد أفلام الكارتون.

ويقضي عمر أجازات نهاية الأسبوع في لعب الكرة، وكرة السلة، والبنج بونج. أما أنا وأصدقائي فنستمع إلى الموسيقى، ونلعب مع قططنا، ونشاهد أفلاما، ونكتشف أشياء على شبكة الإنترنت!

Amarna
Life Under
the Sun

مدينتنا كبيرة حقا. نحن لم نر معظمها لأنه يتوجب علينا السير في كل مكان. واحد من جيراننا عنده بيت كبير ولديه حمار.
أما العائلة الملكية فإنهم لا يمشون ولا يركبون الحمار، وإنما يركبون العربات الذهبية التي تجرها الخيول.

ويركب الملك وأسرته وأصدقائه مرتين في اليوم على طول الطريق الملكي الذي يمتد من شمال المدينة إلى جنوبها. وقبل بداية رحلتهم يقوم جنود المشاة بإخلاء الطريق من جميع الناس.

ماما تقول إن الملك يتوقف عند المعابد للاحتفالات وعند القصور للقيام ببعض الأعمال الهامة. وفي المعابد مع العائلة الملكية، هناك الموسيقيون، ولاعبو الأكروبات، والراقصون. وهناك أيضا الحيوانات التي يتم تقديمها كقرابين لإله الشمس. إنه مشهد مذهل وصاخب حقا.

وكل شخص يعرف موعد وصول الملك!

24

لا توجد سيارات كثيرة في قرانا. وعدد قليل من الأشخاص لديهم دراجات نارية تستطيع السير بسهولة في الشوارع الضيقة.

وبعض من أصدقائنا يسكنون بعيدا عن المدرسة، ولكن هذه ليست مشكلة إذ أن الأشخاص الآخرين في الحي يساعدونهم على الوصول إلى المدرسة. والأطفال الآخرون يركبون الدراجة الهوائية إلى المدرسة.

ما زلنا نستعمل الحمير في حمل الأشياء ولكن الكثير من الناس لا يركبونها على الطرق الكبيرة الآن.

يقول أبي إن الطريق الرئيسي الذي يربط قرانا ببعضها هو نفس الطريق الملكي الذي كانوا يستعملونه في المدينة القديمة. الآن لدينا سيارت وشوارع مسفلتة، ولكن أنا وعمر كنا نتمنى لو كان لدينا عربة تجرها الخيول.

وغالبا ما تنطلق الحافلات السياحية صعودا وهبوطا، وهي تحمل السياح من مختلف أنحاء العالم لزيارة المدينة القديمة والمكان الذي نعيش فيه.

Amarna
Life Under
the Sun

معظم الشخصيات الهامة في مصر تعيش في مدينتنا. والملك هو المسؤول الأول، فلديه قوة آتون وهو إله على الأرض! والملكة نفرتيتي هي إلهة نوعا ما

فهي تساعد الملك في الحفاظ على النظام في الكون من خلال أداء الطقوس وتقديم القرابين لإله الشمس. والعائلة الملكية لديها أربعة قصور.

أما الأمير توت عنخ آمون، فهو سيصبح ملكا في يوم ما ولكنه لا يزال صغيرا ولا يستطيع المساعدة! والملك والملكة عندهم ست بنات. وهؤلاء الأميرات يساعدن والديهم في خدمة إله الشمس. والوزير الأعظم هو المسؤول الثاني في البلاد. فهو يقوم بكل الوظائف الإدارية التي لا يملك الملك الوقت للقيام بها.

وهناك وزير يعيش في مدينتنا، ووزير آخر يعيش في مدينة ممفيس. والكاهن الأكبر مسؤول عن معابد إله الشمس، والمشرفون يديرون الأشياء الهامة مثل مخازن الحبوب والماشية. وهناك فرق من الكتبة يساعدونهم في أعمالهم.

الآن يوجد في قرانا مزارعون، ومدرسون، وأطباء، ومهندسون، وصيادون، ورجال شرطة، وجنود.

ومعظم القرى كان لديها عمدة، وهو بمثابة زعيم محلي يساعد في حكم المنطقة. ولا يزال لدينا أشخاص محترمون نذهب إليهم للحصول على المشورة.

كما أننا نحاول أن نتخذ قراراتنا كمجتمع ولدينا مجلس محلي. لقد علمنا آباؤنا اثنى عشر جيلا من أسماء عائلتنا.

وهذه الأسماء تربطنا بتاريخنا ونحن نعرف حتى المنازل التي عاش فيها أجدادنا وأسلافنا. ونحن نفخر بالرابطة الطويلة التي تربطنا بالمكان الذي نعيش فيه.

Amarna
Life Under
the Sun

الموت والحياة بعد الموت

في معظم الأيام، يمكننا أن نرى الغبار الحجري على المنحدرات الشرقية حيث يتم نحت الصخور لعمل مقابر للملك وأصدقائه.

ويستغرق الأمر سنوات للانتهاء من عمل المقبرة الصخرية، ولكل واحدة منها تصميم مختلف. وقبل دفنهم، سيتم تحنيط هؤلاء الأشخاص.

كما سيتم أيضا وضع الأثاث، والملابس المصنوعة من الكتان، والأطعمة، والتمائم، وتابوت كبير والأشياء الأخري التي سيحتاجونها للحياة الأخرى.

ولكن مدافن جيراننا أسهل من ذلك بكثير حيث أننا نحفر قبرا في الصحراء عند قاعدة المنحدرات. كما نقوم بلف الميت بالكتان أو بحصيرة ونضعهم في قبورهم مع بعض الموتى للحياة الأخرى، مثل بعض جرار الجعة، وقطع من الفاكهة.

ولدينا أحيانا أعياد لتذكر الموتى حيث نتمنى لهم حياة طيبة بعد الموت. كما نأمل أيضا أن يحمونا في هذه الحياة.

28

عندما يموت شخص في قريتنا يقوم فرد من الأسرة بتغسيله ولف جثمانه في كفن أبيض نظيف، ثم يُحمل الجثمان إلى المسجد.

وفي المسجد، يؤم الإمام المصلين في صلاة الجنازة ولدينا عادات خاصة للحداد مدتها أربعون يوما.

وتحتوي الجبانات الإسلامية على مقابر مبنية من الحجر أو الطوب اللبن ذات أسطح مقببة، ولكن أحيانا ما تدفن الجثث مباشرة داخل الأرض في اتجاه مكة المكرمة.

ونحن نتذكر موتانا بزيارة مقابرهم، كل سنة، في ذكرى وفاتهم. ونأخذ معنا طعاما نعطية للفقراء كرحمة على الموتى. هناك أيضا العديد من الأسر المسيحية في مصر الوسطى. وللمسيحيين المصريين غالبا مقابر أسرية في جباناتهم يتم بناؤها بطريقة تشبه مقابرالمقببة.

الملك إله قوي للغاية. لديه إمبراطورية ضخمة لأن جيشه هو الأفضل وقد جعله هذا أغنى شخص في العالم!

وتوفر الثروة الموجودة هنا فرصا للأشخاص المستعدين للعمل الشاق، ولكن بعض هذه الأعمال شاقة ومستنزفة جسديا تحت الشمس الحارقة، خاصة في المحاجر ومواقع البناء. نحن صغار وهذا المكان موطننا. وإنه لأمر مثير أن تكون جزءا من كل كبير. ونحن نحب منزلنا وكل المعابد والقصور الرائعة التي بناها الملك هنا. والكثير من أفراد أسرتنا مدفونون أيضا هنا.

وسوف نحزن بشدة إذا كنا مضطرين إلى مغادرة هذا المكان، أو إذا تهدم منزلنا. ونتمنى أن يهتم أشخاص آخرون بهذه المدينة العظيمة في المستقبل وألا ينسوا قصتنا.

الملك أمنحوتب الثالث – الملكة تي

الملك إخناتون – الملكة نفرتيتي
(الذي كان معروفا بآمنحوتب
الرابع وهو صغير)

بنات إخناتون ونفرتيتي الست

مريت آتون | مكت آتون | عنخ أس أن با آتون | نفر نفرو آتون-تا شريت
نفر نفرو رع | ستبن رع

ابن إخناتون توت عنخ آمون

إن والدة توت عنخ آمون غير معروفة.
فربما تكون نفرتيتي، أو ربما تكون
إحدى زوجات إخناتون الأخريات
(إذ كان لديه أكثر من زوجة، ولكن
نفرتيتي كانت أهمهن).

سؤال البحث!

السؤال الأول: ما الذي يمكنكم معرفته عن نفرتيتي؟ هل نعرف كيف كان شكلها؟ هل هناك أية آثار أو قطع أثرية مرتبطة بها؟ هل عاشت حتى عمر متقدم؟ لماذا، في رأيكم، لا تزال مشهورة جدا؟ أين يمكنكم الذهاب لرؤية نفرتيتي اليوم؟ هل يمكنكم العثور على أية أمثلة لصورة لنفرتيتي تُستخدم في الإعلانات أو كشعار لشركة؟ هل تعرفون أية امرأة قوية أخرى من مصر القديمة؟

السؤال الثاني: تل العمارنة مدينة مشهورة للعديد من الأسباب، ليس فقط بسبب أشخاص مثل نفرتيتي! إن أول دليل على اختراع مهم يسمى "الشادوف" معروف من تل العمارنة. هل يمكنكم معرفة ما هو الشادوف؟ ومما يُصنع؟ وكيف يعمل؟ هل يشبه اي شيء نستعمله اليوم؟ هل يمكنكم أن تجدوا اختراعات أخرى من مصر القديمة؟

بعض الأماكن الجيدة لبدء البحث عن إجابة هذه الأسئلة هي المتاحف، والمكتبات، والإنترنت. يمكنكم أيضا أن تسألوا أحد الأثريين!

نشاط 2: رياضيات الجسم

لقد اعتمدت المقاييس المصرية القديمة على أجزاء الجسم، وكان الذراع هو وحدة القياس الأكثر استخداما. وهو مقدار المسافة بين كوع الشخص البالغ وأطراف أصابعه (حوالي 52.5سم)

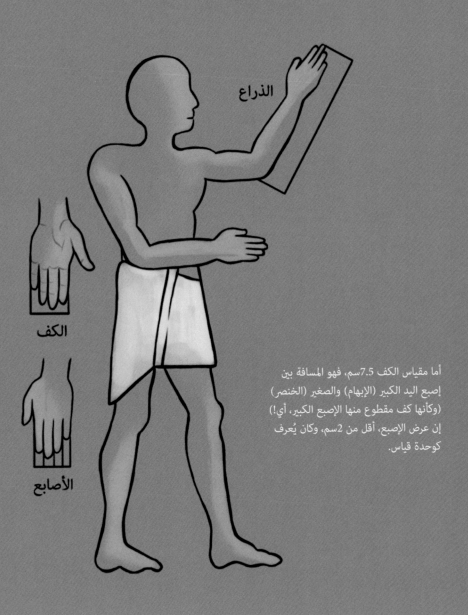

الذراع

الكف

الأصابع

أما مقياس الكف 7.5سم، فهو المسافة بين إصبع اليد الكبير (الإبهام) والصغير (الخنصر) (وكأنها كف مقطوع منها الإصبع الكبير، أي!) إن عرض الإصبع، أقل من 2سم، وكان يُعرف كوحدة قياس.

هذا مقياس الذراع الملكي الطويل. إنه يشبه المسطرة. إن طوله ذراع واحد (حوالي 52.5سم) وهو مقسم إلى سبعة أكف كل منها أربعة أصابع، مما يجعل المجموع ثمانية وعشرين إصبعا. وقد استخدم المعماريون الذراع الملكي الطويل في رسم المباني الكبيرة – مثل المعابد في مدينة تل العمارنة القديمة.

هل تعرفون أن الناس ما زالوا يقيسون الأشياء بأجزاء من الجسم في العديد من البلدان حول العالم إلى الآن؟ فمقياس القدم الحديث مقداره 30سم، وهو طول قدم الرجل البالغ تقريبا. ومن المحتمل أن اليونانيين هم أول من استعملوا هذا المقياس.

سؤال القياس!

هل تستطيعون قياس الأشياء من حولكم باستخدام المقاييس المصرية القديمة؟

ما هو طولك بالذراع، والكف، والإصبع؟

ما مدى اتساع الغرفة التي توجد بها الآن؟

ما هي الأشياء الأخرى التي تود قياسها؟

نشاط 3: الكتابة بالخطوط والصور

كان معظم المصريين القدماء أميون لا يعرفون القراءة والكتابة، مما يعني أنه لابد أن يذهبوا إلى أحد **الكتبة** إذا ما أرادوا إرسال خطاب. وهذا الخطاب سيكون مكتوبا على ورق سميك مصنوع من **نبات** البردي. الأغنياء فقط هم الذين يستطيعون إرسال أبنائهم إلى المدارس ليصبحوا كتبة. لقد قام **الكتاب** بكتابة معظم الكتابات في مصر القديمة، ولكن الشخصيات الهامة مثل الكهنة والعائلة الملكية هم أيضا يعرفون القراءة والكتابة.

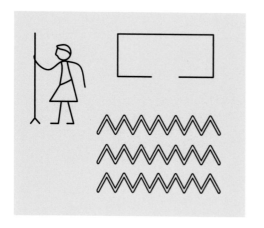

عندما كانت مدينة تل العمارنة هي عاصمة مصر، كان هناك شكلان من الكتابة قيد الاستخدام. الشكل الأول هو الخط الهيروغليفي وتشبه بعض رموز الهيروغليفية صور الأشياء التي تدل عليها. هل ميكنكم رؤية الرمز الهيروغليفي الذي يدل على "رجل عجوز" إنه يشبه تماما الرجل العجوز، وكيف أن رمز كلمة بيت يشبه البيت، ورمز ماء يشبه أمواج المياه؟

وعندما أصبحت اللغة المكتوبة أكثر تعقيدا تم اختراع رموز هيروغليفية جديدة. وتم ربط بعض هذه الرموز بصوت مختلف أو حتى بأصوات قليلة. أما الرموز الجديدة الأخرى فليس لها أصوات تدل عليها ولكنها كانت تُستعمل كعلامات بصرية للمساعدة على شرح المعنى الكامل للكلمة. إن اللغة الهيروغليفية لم تكن مكتوبة في اتجاه معين كما يبدو الأمر منطقيا بالنسبة لنا اليوم – ولكن الرموز غالبا ماكانت مجمعة معا. لقد كانت لغة معقدة للغاية!

لقد كانت الهيروغليفية تُستخدم بشكل أساسي في المعابد وفي مقابر الأثرياء.

أما الشكل الثاني فهو الخط الهيراطيقي، وكان يستخدم أكثر في المهام اليومية مثل كتابة الخطابات وإدارة أعمال الملك. لقد كان الخط الهيراطيقي مستندا إلى الخط الهيروغليفي ولكنه كان أسرع في الكتابة حيث تم تبسيط الرموز.

لم تعد الهيروغليفية والهيراطيقية مستخدمة الآن في مصر أو في أي مكان في العالم. وفي الحقيقة فإن معرفة قراءتها ظلت مجهولة لمدة تزيد عن ألف سنة! ولكن شكل من أشكال اللغة المصرية القديم استمر من خلال اللغة القبطية، والتي ما تزال مستخدمة إلى اليوم في الكنائس المصرية. وتُكتب اللغة القبطية بحروف اللغة اليونانية القديمة مع بعض الرموز الإضافية من الهيروغليفية. ومنذ ما يقرب من مائتي سنة، عندما أصبح العالم مهتما حقا مبصر القدمية، كان العلماء يحاولون قراءة الهيروغليفية وكأنها شفرة سرية. وأخيرا تمكن العالم الفرنسي جان-فرانسوا شامبليون من حل رموز الهيروغليفية سنة 1822.

سؤال اللغة!

هل يمكنكم فك رموز هذه الأسماء الهيروغليفية المبسطة باستخدام الحروف والأصوات المختلفة المبينة في الجدول أسفله؟ إن كل مجموعة من الرموز تكون اسما من أسماء شخصية مشهورة من شخصيات تل العمارنة! وكل اسم مكتوب داخل خرطوش. والخرطوش هو شكل بيضاوي بسطر مكتوب على أحد وجهيه، ويُستخدم عادة لكتابة أسماء الملوك. وفي مدينة تل العمارنة، فإن اسم الإله آتون مكتوب داخل الخراطيش كذلك.

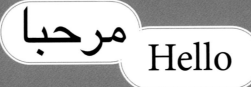

Hello

نصائح للترجمة! اللغة العربية تُكتب من اليمين إلى اليسار مثل كلمة – مرحبا. واللغة الإنجليزية تُكتب من اليسار إلى اليمين مثل كلمة – Hello. أما اللغة الهيروغليفية فيمكن أن تُكتب من اليسار إلى اليمين، أو من اليمين إلى اليسار، أو من أعلى إلى أسفل. ولكنها لا تُكتب أبدا من أسفل إلى أعلى!

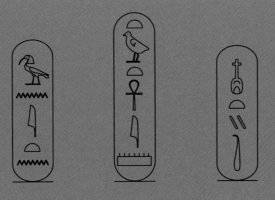

ي	و	تي	ت	ن	نِفِر	مون	نخ	خ	ي (أو ا)

عندما كُتبت هذه الخراطيش الثلاثة، كان بها الكثير من الرموز الإضافية وأحيانا ما تم نقل أجزاء من الأسماء. وهذا يوضح لنا مدى صعوبة تعلم الهجاء في مصر القديمة! هل يمكنكم معرفة الخراطيش التي تتطابق مع الخراطيش التي قمتم للتو بفك رموزها؟

هل يمكن أن تكتب اسمك بهيروغليفية بسيطة؟

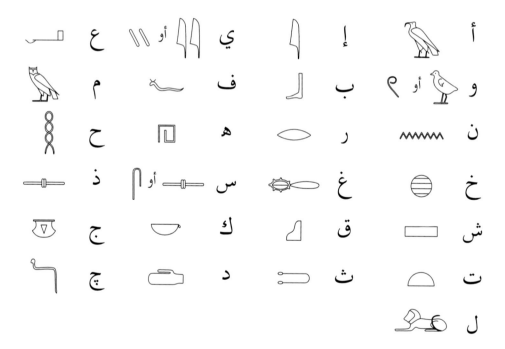

نشاط 4: استكشاف القوى الحامية

هل لديك شيء خاص ترتديه أو تحمله معك أينما ذهبت ليجلب لك الحظ. في مصر القديمة، كان الناس، من مختلف الأعمار، الفقراء والأغنياء، لديهم تعويذة أو تميمة شخصية واحدة على الأقل. وغالبا ما كانت التميمة يتم ارتداؤها كقطعة مجوهرات يمكن صنعها على هيئة أشكال مختلفة وبألوان متعددة ومن مواد مختلفة مثل الزجاج، والخزف، والكتان، والحجر، وحتى الخشب.

وكان من المعتقد أن تصيم له قوى حامية مختلفة. لقد كانت التمائم مهمة للأحياء، ولكنها كانت ضرورية ايضا لحماية الموتى. ولذلك غالبا ما نجدها في لفائف المومياء أو في المدافن حيث توضع مع الجثث قبل الدفن.

وأحيانا ما كان يتم دفن الأشخاص بالتمائم التي كانوا يرتدونها أثناء حياتهم. كما كانت هناك تمائم خاصة كان يتم استخدامها في الدفن فقط لمساعدة اليت في الحياة الأخرى.

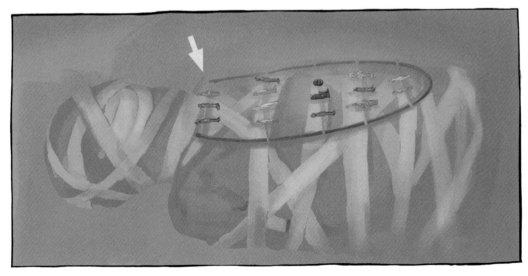

وقد تم العثور على الآلاف من التمائم ذات القوى الحامية المختلفة أثناء الحفريات الأثرية (التنقيب) في تل العمارنة.

عين الوجات

عين الوجات
إن التصميم الأكثر شيوعا للمجوهرات أو للتمائم في تل العمارنة هو عين الوجات. وتربط القصص المصرية القديمة هذه العين بالإله حورس الذي فقد إحدى عينيه في معركة مع إله آخر يُدعى ست. وربما كانت للعين قوى حامية وكان يتم ارتداؤها في الحياة والموت. إن علامة العين موجودة في اللغة الهيروغليفية. وعندما تقال بصوت عال فسوف تكون كلمة تشبه وجات.

بس
كان الإله بس أحد آلهة مصر القديمة. وكانت وظيفته الرئيسية حماية الأمهات والأطفال. وعادة ما كان يصور على هيئة رجل متقزم يرتدي قناعا مخيفا. وفي بعض الأحيان كان يُصور بلبدة الأسد وذيله وفي يديه دف. وقد تم العثور على الكثير من التمائم الصغيرة وقطع المجوهرات على شكل الإله بس في تل العمارنة. وقد كان يتم ارتداؤها خاصة من قبل النساء والأطفال الذين عاشوا هناك لحمايتهم من العين.

الإله بس

خنفساء الجعل
كما كانت التمائم على شكل خنفساء الجعل شائعة أيضا في مصر القديمة. وقد كانت مرتبطة بالإله خبري وغالبا ما كان يتم تصويره على هيئة جسم رجل ورأس خنفساء. وعادة ما كان الجزء السفلي المسطح من تمائم الجعل مزينة بصور أو كتابات هيروغليفية. والجعل مرتبط بالبعث وغالبا ما يوجد في المدافن.

خنفساء الجعل

وأيضا تم العثور على الكثير من التمائم على شكل سمكة في تل العمارنة. وقد كانت السمكة رمزا آخر للبعث وكانت تُستخدم في الدفن. ومن المعتقد أيضا أن التمائم على هيئة الأسماك توفر الحماية أثناء الحياة، خصوصا للأطفال!

سؤال التصميم!

والآن أنت خبير في التمائم! ويمكنك تصميم التميمة الخاصة بك. كيف سيكون شكلها؟ هل ستكون على شكل حيوان، أو نبات، أو شخص، أو شيء آخر مختلف تماما؟ وما هو لونها؟ وما هي القوة الحامية التي لديها؟ لماذا اخترت هذا الشكل لتميمتك؟

نشاط 5: السفر على الطريق الملكي

لم يكن الطريق الملكي طريقا عاديا. فهو يمتد في قلب مدينة أخت آتون من الشمال إلى الجنوب، وقد اصطف على جانبيه أهم المباني في المدينة. وربما استخدم هذا الطريق العمال الذين يسيرون على أقدامهم أو الذين يركبون الحمير، بالإضافة إلى المسؤولين في العربات التي تجرها الخيول. ولكن أهم رحلة خلال اليوم كانت تلك التي يقوم بها الملك وحاشيته.

ومرتان في اليوم، كان إخناتون يقود عربته الذهبية على الطريق الملكي. وكان ينضم إليه في هذه الرحلة بقية العائلة الملكية وحراسه الملكيين.

وكان من المعتقد أن الملك هو إله حي على الأرض. فهو ممثل إله الشمس، آتون. وكان الملك مرتبطا بالإله آتون من خلال الطريق الملكي. وعندما يسافر الملك من الشمال إلى الجنوب على الطريق تحت أشعة الشمس الساطعة، فإن الإله آتون (الشمس) يتحرك من الشرق إلى الغرب في السماء. وفي طريقه، كان إخناتون يتوقف للعبادة في معابد المدينة، أو ليعتني بالأعمال المهمة.

وفي داخل المعابد، كان المسؤولون الكبار، والراقصون، والموسيقيون يستقبلون الملك. كما كان يتم تقديم الماشية كقرابين لإله الشمس. وكانت مشاهد وأصوات وروائح جميع الأشخاص والأنشطة المختلفة التي تجري داخل أراضي المعبد مثابة مشهد رائع!

وإلى الآن، ما زال بإمكانكم السير على جزء من الطريق الملكي! فالجزء الأكثر حفظا هو ذلك الذي يمر عبر معابد وقصور المدينة المركزية المدمرة.

سؤال الخيال!

تخيل أنك عامل في أحد المعابد عندما يمر الملك في موكبه على الطريق الملكي. اكتب بطاقة بريدية لصديق تشرح فيها كيف يبدو المنظر. ما هو دورك أثناء زيارة الملك؟ هل أنت كاهن، ، أو راقص، أو موسيقي، أو ربما الشخص المسؤول عن الحيوانات التي تُقدم كقرابين لإله الشمس؟ ماذا يمكنك أن ترى؟ ماذا يمكنك أن تشم؟ ماذا يمكنك أن تسمع؟ كيف تشعر؟ ما هو رأيك في الملك والعائلة الملكية؟ ارسم صورة في مقدمة البطاقة البريدية لتوضح بها وصفك.

نشاط6: إنتاج الأنماط

كان أسوب الفن في تل العمارنة قديما مميزا جدا. ويبدو أن استخدام الأشكال الأكثر ليونة والاهتمام بالتفاصيل جعلا الصور أكثر حيوية مقارنة بأوقات سابقة. فإخناتون وعائلته يحتضنون بعضهم البعض، كما في صورة عائلية. والجنود المشاة، والراقصون، والمسافرون في العربات السريعة يبدو وكأنهم قد يخرجون من المشاهد المرسومة في أية لحظة! والنباتات والأشجار تهتز بفعل الرياح. والطيور تبدو جاهزة للطيران، والخيول جاهزة للركض، وتقفز العجول عبر النهر.

كانت النباتات، والطيور، والحيوانات مهمة جدا للمصريين القدماء فهي تظهر القوة الواهبة لإله الشمس – آتون. وقد استخدم الفنانون الأشكال، والأنماط، والألوان التي رأوها في الطبيعة في تزيين المعابد، والمقابر، والبيوت.

ولقد أحب المصريون القدماء استخدام الألوان الزاهية. فالأحمر، والأزرق، والأصفر، والأخضر، والأبيض كانت الألوان الرئيسية المستخدمة في تل العمارنة. وتم تزيين جدران، وأسقف، وأحيانا أرضيات المنازل المهمة (وخاصة القصور الملكية) بزهور الأقحوان، وزهور اللوتس، ونبات البردي في مناظر لحياة النهر أو أنماط لافتة للنظر.

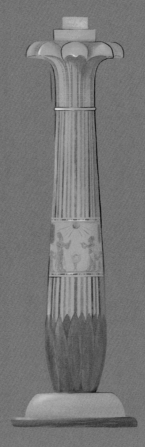

وغالبا ما كانت الأعمدة الحجرية في تل العمارنة على شكل نباتات وقمتها مزينة بأوراق نخيل البلح، أو أوراق البردي. وأحيانا كانت تتم إضافة عناقيد العنب إلى التصميم، بالإضافة إلى الطيور المائية، والفراشات، والأسماك، والزهور البرية.

وقد ألهمت الزهور، والفواكه، والبتلات، والنباتات الأخري تصميم القلادات والأواني الفخارية. وقد تم تصنيعها في ورش تقع بالقرب من مركز المدينة القديمة، وعلى أطراف المنطقة السكنية. ففي بعض الورش، كان الفنانون ينحتون التماثيل من الحجر، وفي البعض الآخر كانوا يصنعون المجوهرات من المعادن النفيسة أو يحولون كتل الفخار إلى أواني جميلة.

وقام الناس أيضا بصناعة اشياء صغيرة كالمجوهرات والأدوات في بيوتهم. فقد كان عليهم أن يكونوا مكتفين ذاتيا في مصر القديمة – إذا كنت بحاجة إلى شيء، فعليك أن تصنعه بنفسك!

سؤال الفن!

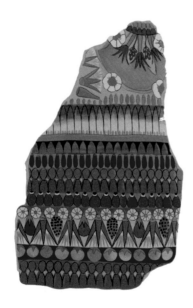

يتكون النمط من تصميم متكرر من الألوان والأشكال. والكثير من الأنماط التي ابتكرها الفنانون والحرفيون في تل العمارنة كانت متماثلة او ذات زخارف متكررة. ما هي الأنماط التي تراها حولك في الحياة اليومية؟ ماهي النباتات، والحيوانات، والأشكال، والألوان التي تفضلها؟ لماذا لا تجمع بين الأشياء المفضلة لديك من الطبيعة لتصنع نمط التكرار الخاص بك مستلهما التصاميم من تل العمارنة القديمة؟ يمكنك أن تستخدم النمط الخاص بك كزخرفة لوعاء أو كلوحة لمنزلك!

نشاط 7: صنع الخبز وتخمير الجعة

بالنسبة للكثير من المصريين القدماء، تمحورت الحياة حول الزراعة. وقد كانت هناك حاجة لمحاصيل الحبوب مثل القمح، والشعير لصنع الطعام والشراب الأكثر أهمية – الخبز والجعة الخفيفة جدا! فكل شخص في تل العمارنة القديمة من الملك إلى أفقر العائلات كانت وجبته تحتوي على هذين البندين.

وكان الخبز والجعة قرابينا هامة للآلهة في المعابد. ففي تل العمارنة القديمة، كان هناك مخبزا ضخما بجوار معبد آتون الكبير ينتج خبزا لإله الشمس. وفي الحياة الأخرى، كانت هناك أيضا حاجة إلى أرغفة الخبز وجرار الجعة. وأحيانا كانت توضع داخل المقابر، أو كانت مناظر صنع الخبز وتخمير الجعة تُرسم على جدران المقابر.

لا يزال الخبز من أكثر الأطعمة التي يتم تناولها بشكل واسع في كل أنحاء العالم. والمكون الرئيسي عادة هو القمح. وهناك عدة أنواع من القمح. فاليوم، هناك نوع من القمح يُستخدم لصنع الخبز، ونوع آخر لصنع المكرونة. وقد استخدم المصريون القدماء نوعا آخر من القمح يسمى قمح الإمر والذي لا يكاد يُزرع اليوم. ويحتوي هذا النوع على غلاف صلب يغلف حبة القمح ويتطلب الكثير من العمل الشاق لإزالته. وقد قام المصريون القدماء بذلك عن طريق دق الحبوب بأداة خشبية خاصة في وعاء حجري كبير لكسر الغلاف وفصله عن الحبوب. وبعد ذلك، كانوا يطحنون الحبوب لعمل الدقيق.

وعندما يصبح الدقيق جاهزا، يتم إضافة الماء لصنع العجين. ويمكن إضافة مكونات أخرى كثيرة من أجل النكهة، مثل البذور والزيت. ومعظم الخبز المصري القديم والحديث مسطح، وذلك لأنه يُخبز بدون خميرة. والخميرة هي نوع خاص من الفطريات الصالحة للأكل والتي تجعل الخبز منتفخا وتمنحه مذاقا خاصا. لقد كانت الخميرة تُضاف إلى بعض أنواع الخبز المصري القديم، ولكن لم تكن تُستخدم دائما.

لابد من خبز الخبز قبل تناوله. وفي مصر القديمة، كان الخبز يتم خبزه على النار أو على ألواح حجرية موضوعة فوق النار. وفي تل العمارنة كان الكثير من البيوت بها أفران على شكل قبة. وكانت هذه الأفران مصنوعة من الطين. لم يكن هناك كهرباء في مصر القديمة: ولكي يسخنوا الأفران، كان لابد أن يشعلوا نارا داخلها. وعندما تسخن جدران الفرن تتم إزالة بقايا النار.

وبعد ذلك، يتم مسح داخل الفرن بفرشاة أو قطعة قماش مبللة للتخلص من السخام. وبينما يقوم أحد الأشخاص بفعل ذلك، يقوم شخص آخر بتقريص العجين. ثم بعد ذلك يُفرد العجين، ويُفرك أسفله بالماء أو باللبن ويرمى إلى داخل الفرن الساخن. إن ما تبقى من حرارة النار سيؤدي إلى تسوية الخبز. ويصبح الخبز جاهزا عندما يرتفع بعيدا عن جوانب الفرن وتبدأ رائحته الخاصة تملأ الهواء.

سؤال الخبز

لماذا لا تحاول صنع الخبز المُخمر المصري القديم الخاص بك؟ تأكد من طلب المساعدة من شخص كبير! هذه الوصفة تكفي لأربعة أرغفة صغيرة أو رغيف واحد كبير.

ضع معا في وعاء كبير:

- 250ج دقيق سادة
- 180مل ماء دافئ
- حفنة ملح
- 5ج خميرة (5ج عادة هي مقدار عبوة صغيرة من ا. لخميرة. لم يكن لدى المصريين القدماء أكياس من الخميرة. ربما قاموا بالاحتفاظ ببعض العجين المخمر في كل مرة يصنعون فيها الخبز، لذا فالخليط التالي سيحتوي على الخميرة التي تجعله ينفش. ولأن الخميرة حية، فهي يمكن أن تنمو وتتضاعف في العجين الجديد)

ستحتاج أيضا إلى:

- قطعة قماش قطنية صغيرة (يمكن أيضا أن نستعمل البلاستيك الواقي ولكنه لم يكن موجودا في مصر القديمة!)

يُعجن الخليط في الوعاء لمدة خمس دقائق على الأقل، مُده إلى الخارج ثم اضغط عليه إلى أسفل بيديك. إذا كان طريا جدا، أضف القليل من الدقيق. وإذا كان جافا جدا، أضف المزيد من الماء.

غطي الوعاء بقطعة قماش قطنية صغيرة واترك العجين ليتخمر في مكان دافئ قليلا (ليس في الثلاجة) لمدة تتراوح بين ساعة وساعتين حتي يتضاعف حجمه. قد يتشقق السطح قليلا.

اعجن العجين مرة أخرى وشكله كما تريد. ربما تريد أن تقسمه إلى أرغفة صغيرة، أو تصنع منه رغيفا كبيرا. لقد كان الخبز في مصر القديمة مستديرا أو مثلثا. وأحيانا كان على شكل سمكة، أو حيوان، أو جسم بشري. يمكنك أن تجرب هذا وتنتظر النتيجة. ضع أشكالك على ورقة خبز مدهونة واتركها لمدة ساعة لترتفع مرة أخرى.

والآن خبزك جاهز للفرن. لا تقلق إذا لم يكن لديك فرن مصنوع من الطين. إذا كان لديك فرن يعمل بالغاز أو الكهرباء فليست هناك مشكلة! تأكد من أن الفرن يعمل بشكل جيد وأنه ساخن (درجة الحرارة المناسبة هي 220 مئوية/400 فهرنهايت). وسيعتمد الوقت الذي سيستغرقه الخبز ليصبح جاهزا على حجم الرغيف (حوالي 10 دقائق للأرغفة الصغيرة و30 دقيقة للأرغفة الكبيرة). وستعرف أنه قد اصبح جاهزا عندما ينتفخ الخبز، ويتحول لونه إلى اللون الذهبي-البني.

نحن لا نعرف بالضبط ماذا كان المصريون القدماء يأكلون مع الخبز – ربما لا شيء إذا كانوا فقراء أو إذا كانوا يريدون وجبة سريعة! وللوجبة الرئيسية، فربما يتناولون الخضروات مثل البصل، أوالسبانخ، أوالجزر، أو العدس مع الخبز، أو السمك من النيل. وإذا كانوا أكثر ثراء، فربما كانوا يأكلون لحم الماعز أو الماشية.

نشاط 8: البناء بالطين والحجر

استخدمت التربة (الطين) في بناء الأشياء لآلاف السنين. فالتربة في كل مكان تقريبا، مما يعني أنه من السهل العثور عليها. وعندما يتم مزجها بالماء ومواد أخرى يمكن استخدامها بطرق كثيرة. والمشكلة الكبيرة في المباني المبنية بالطين هي أنها يمكن أن تُتلف بسهولة وتحتاج إلى إصلاح منتظم.

كانت معظم المباني في تل العمارنة القديمة مبنيه من الطوب اللبن. أما الأجزاء الأكثر أهمية في المدينة – مثل المعابد – فقد كانت مبنية من الحجر. وكان يتم تقطيع الحجارة إلى كتل صغيرة تُسمى "تلاتات" في المحاجر القريبة. وقد تم تصميم الكتل ليحملها شخص قوي. انظروا مرة أخرى إلى سؤال القياس لمعرفة حجم حجر التلاتات. إن طوله ذراع، وعرضه نصف ذراع، وسمكه نصف ذراع. هل تعتقد أنك قوي بما فيه الكفاية لتحمل واحدا من هذه الأحجار؟

وقد تم استخدام الطوب اللبن في بناء جميع المنازل في تل العمارنة القديمة، بما في ذلك قصر الملك! فالطوب اللبن أرق وأخف وزنا بكثير من الكتل الحجرية كما يختلف حجمه على حسب طريقة صنعه. وفي تل العمارنة، بلغ طول الطوبة اللبنية 34سم، وعرضها 17سم، وسمكها 8سم.

وكان أفضل طوب لبن هو ذلك المصنوع من التربة القريبة من النيل. وكان يتم خلطه بالرمل والحصى من الصحراء، ثم يضاف الماء للمساعدة في تثبيته. ثم يوضع خليط الطوب اللبن في قالب خشبي على شكل مستطيل لإعطائه الشكل الصحيح. وبعد ذلك يُرفع القالب وتُترك الطوبة في الشمس لتجف.

ولبناء جدار، كان الطوب يوضع في أنماط متداخلة، مما يساعد على جعل الجدار أقوى. ثم يُثبت الطوب في مكانه بطبقة مبللة من الطين تسمى الملاط. وعندما يجف الطين تصبح قوالب الطوب متماسكة معا.

ومجرد الانتهاء من بناء جدار يتم تغطيته بطبقة من الملاط من
الداخل والخارج. وهذا الملاط مصنوع أيضا من الطين، حيث يتم
تحويل الطين إلى عجين بالماء، ثم تُضاف إليه أجزاء من القش حتى
لا يتشقق الملاط. وفي تل العمارنة القديمة، تم دهان بعض المنازل
من الداخل باللون الأبيض. وفي المنازل الأوسع، التي يمكلها الأشخاص
المهمين في المدينة، وُضعت أحيانا لوحات ملونة على الجدران،
والأسقف، وحول الأبواب، كما رأيتم في نشاط إنتاج الأنماط.

وكانت الأبواب والنوافذ مصنوعة من الخشب أو الحجر، وغالبا ما
كانت تُطلى باللون الأحمر. أما الأرضيات فقد تكون مصنوعة من
الملاط أو الطوب، ولكنها غالبا ما كانت مجرد أرض طبيعية ممهدة
ومستوية نتيجة رش المياه والدوس الأقدام.

وقد كانت الأسطح مستوية وعادة ما كانت مدعومة بعوارض خشبية
مثبتة بأعمدة في الغرف الأكبر. وكان يتم تغطية هذه العوارض
بالحصير أو مواد نباتية وطبقة من الطين. وإذا كان السطح قويا
بدرجة كافية، يمكن إضافة طابق ثان للمنزل.

والطوب اللبن هو عازل جيد. فهو يساعد على إبقاء المنازل باردة في
الصيف، ودافئة في الشتاء. ونظرا لعدم وجود دفايات أو مكيفات
للهواء في مصر القديمة، فقد كان هذا مهما للغاية!

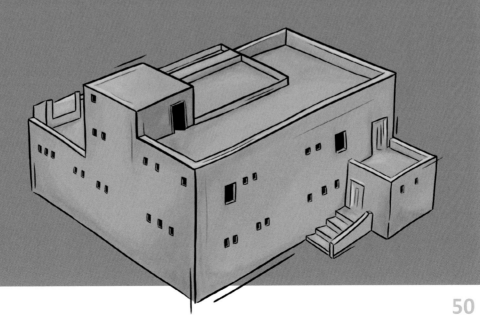

هل يمكنك اتباع الطريقة المصرية القديمة لتقوم بصنع الطوب اللبن الخاص بك؟ ربما يمكنك إضافة كميات مختلفة من الرمل، أو الحصى، أو القش لخليط الطين لمعرفة ما الذي يجعل الطوب أقوى؟ يمكنك اختبار قوة الطوبة من خلال وضع نهاياتها على فجوة بين صندوقين من البلاستيك. أضف تدريجيا الأوزان الصغيرة إلى منتصف الطوبة، وانتظر لترى كم من الوقت تستغرقه قبل ان تنكسر. تأكد من أن أصابع قدميك ليست في الطريق عندما تنكسر الطوبة!

سوف تحتاج إلى:

- صندوق بلاستيك صغير يمكن عمل فتحات به وسوف يكون بمثابة قالب الطوب. لم يعرف المصريون القدماء البلاستيك لأنه لم يكن قد تم اختراعه بعد. لقد كانت قوالبهم مصنوعة من الخشب. وبالنسبة لتجربتنا، تعتبر علب الحلاوة البلاستيكية مثالية، ولكن شيئا أكبر أو أصغر قليلا يمكن أن يكون جيدا كذلك!

- الكثير من التربة الناعمة (الطين) (أحضروا شخصا يرتدي قفازات للتأكد للتأكد من عدم وجود أشياء حادة في الطين)

- ماء

- مقص مسنون (اطلب من شخص كبير المساعدة في ذلك)

- كمية جيدة من الرمل و/أو الحصى (الزلط) - يمكنك أيضا استخدام بعض القش المفروم إذا كان متوافرا لديك

- وعاء كبير مثل دلو بلاستيك أو صفيحة قمامة

خطوة 1: قم بتحضير التربة عن طريق تفتيت الكتل الكبيرة وإزالة الأحجار الكبيرة أو قطع الأغصان.

خطوة 2: استخدموا عصا لخلط التربة بالماء في الوعاء الكبير لتكوين طين سميك (يجب أن يكون مبتلا بدرجة كافية ليكون متماسكا - تقريبا مثل عجينة الخبز!).

خطوة 3: أضف حفنات قليلة من الرمل، والحصى، و/أو القش (وتسمى هذه الإضافات بالخليط) حتى لا يتشقق الطوب.

خطوة 4: اخلط الطين والخليط معا بشكل جيد.

خطوة 5: استخدم المقص لعمل عدد من الفتحات في قاع الوعاء البلاستيك لتسمح بدخول الهواء (سيؤدي هذا إلى عدم التصاق الخليط بقاع الوعاء). اطلب من شخص كبير أن يساعدك في استعمال المقص، وانتبه لأصابعك! وبعد ذلك ضع الخليط في الوعاء. تأكد من ملء قوالب الطوب إلى أعلى ثم اضغطها إلى أسفل بإحكام. سوف يساعد هذا على جعل السطح مستويا وإزالة أية فقاعات هوائية.

خطوة 6: اقلب القالب على الفور وبسرعة ولكن بحرص على لوح من الخشب أو أي سطح مغطى برمل أو قش (حتى لا يلتصق!). وبرفق ارفع الوعاء البلاستيك ليصبح جاهزا لقالب الطوب التالي. وإذا بدأ قالب الطوب في الترهل أو التضاؤل فالخليط رطب جدا. حاول إضافة المزيد من التربة. وإذا بدأ قالب الطوب في الانهيار والتفتت فالخليط جاف جدا. حاول إضافة القليل من الماء.

خطوة 7: دع الطوب يجف في الشمس (يجب أن تظل صبورا – قد يأخذ هذا عدة ايام أو حتى أسابيع!). سوف تعرف أن الطوب قد أصبح جاهزا عندما يتغير لونه إلى البني الفاتح أو الرمادي وعندما تشعر بأنه جاف تماما حين تلمسه.

بعد جفاف الطوب، يصبح جاهزا للإستخدام في تجارب القوة. ما هي استنتاجاتك؟ ما هو الخليط الأفضل؟ ما هي كمية الخليط الأحسن التي يمكن إضافتها لجعل الطوب أقوى؟ ما مقدار الوزن الذي يمكن أن تتحمله قوالبك؟ هل يمكن أن تثق في الطوب الخاص بك لبناء جدار؟

نشاط 9: صنع القماش والأزياء

تماما مثل اليوم: كانت الملابس والمنسوجات (الأقمشة) مهمة في كل مناحي الحياة في مصر القديمة. وفي تل العمارنة يمكننا قول الكثير عن الأشياء التي كان الناس يرتدونها من خلال رؤية المناظر المرسومة على جدران المقابر والمعابد. وقد عثر الأثريون أيضا على بقايا العديد من المنسوجات المختلفة حينما كانو يقومون بعمليات التنقيب في المنازل والجبانات.

الكتان، الذي يُصنع من نبات الكتان، كان القماش الأكثر استخداما في مصر القديمة. كما تم أيضا استخدام صوف الغنم، وشعر الماعز، وألياف لحاء النخيل لصنع الأقمشة.

وقد تم صنع الخيوط أو خيوط الغزل من ألياف نباتية أو حيوانية عن طريق الغزل، من خلال جدل الكثير من الألياف الرفيعة معا لعمل خيوط أكثر طولا وسمكا. بعد ذلك يتم لف هذه الخيوط في كرات. وأحيانا ما كان يتم تبييض هذه الخيوط عن طريق غسلها وتجفيفها في الشمس. كما يمكن أيضا تلوينها باستخدام أصباغ مأخوذة من النباتات ومواد طبيعية أخرى ، ولكن معظم الملابس كانت مصنوعة من خيوط غير مصبوغة ولم يتم تبييضها. وعندما يصبح الخيط جاهزا، يمكن نسجه وتحويله إلى قطعة قماش على النول.

والنول هو أداة كبيرة للنسج. ويتم تثبيت الخيط في أحد طرفيه، ثم يمرر الخيط تحت وفوق الخيوط الثابتة لعمل شبكة مترابطة تسمى النسيج.

واليوم نحن نستخدم الآلات لنسج الأقمشة، ولكن في مصر القديمة كان ذلك يتم يدويا. وكان هناك نوعان من الأنوال في تل العمارنة. الأول يمكن استخدامه في وضع مستقيم مثبت على قواعد على الأرض أو مستندا على الحائط. والنوع الآخر يوضع على الأرض ويثبت على عوارض خشبية مرتفعة قليلا عن الأرض. وقد كان النول المستقيم منتشرا في تل العمارنة القديمة لأنه كان مناسبا أكثر لعمل قطع القماش الكبيرة. وقد أدى هذا إلى ظهور موضة جديدة للثنيات والطيات في ملابس الأثرياء.

سؤال التكنولوجيا!

لماذا لا تنسج القماش الخاص بك؟ سوف تحتاج إلى:

- قطعة واحدة صغيرة من الورق المقوى (من صندوق كرتون مثلا، مربع بحجم 12سم x 12سم ، ويمكنك زيادة الحجم!).
- قلم جاف أو رصاص
- مقص
- كرة صغيرة من الصوف أو الخيط، أو عدة أطوال من الخيوط الصوفية أو الملونة
- مسطرة
- شريط لاصق
- إبرة نسيج (وهذه ليست ضرورية كما هو موضح أدناه)

خطوة 1: استخدم المسطرة لترسم خطا على كل جانب من جانبي قطعة الورق المقوى. يجب أن يكون كل خط على بعد 2سم تقريبا من حافة النول إلى الداخل.

خطوة 2: على طول هذين الجانبين المتقابلين، ارسم خطوطا للفتحات، بحيث تكون المسافة بين كل خط والآخر حوالي 0.5 سم.

خطوة 3: بعناية، اقطع على طول هذه الخطوط التي رسمتها للفتحات، وقف عند الخطين المتقابلين.

خطوة 4: خذ خيطا قويا والصقه على الجزء الخلفي من النول (الجانب الذي لم توضع علامة عليه). مرر الخيط خلال الفتحة الأولى في الجزء العلوي الأيسر من قطعة الورق المقوى، ولفه على مقدمة النول ومن خلال الفتحة المقابلة في أسفل قطعة الورق المقوى. استمر في القيام بذلك (كما في الصورة الموجودة في الصفحة التالية) وعند النهاية الصق الخيط على الجزء الخلفي أيضا.

خطوة 5: قص طول جديد من الخيط (حوالي 2 ذراع). يمكنك إما أن تضع الخيط في إبرة نسيج (وعمل عقدة حتى لا يسقط الخيط)، أو لف قطعة صغيرة من الشريط اللاصق حول نهاية الخيط - مما يجعلها أكثر صلابة – ثم انسج به مباشرة.

وفي تل العمارنة، كان النسيج يُصنع في ورش وكذلك في المنازل. وكانت الكلت منتشرة بين الرجال الأغنياء، بينما كانت النساء من الأسر الثرية يلفون أنفسهن بقطعة كبيرة من القماش مثبتة بواسطة عقدة أو حزام. وفي بعض الأحيان كانت ملابس الأثرياء مطوية ومزينة بشبكة مهدبة أو حتى مصبوغة أو منسوجة بألوان زاهية.

أما أفراد الأسر الفقيرة من الرجال والنساء في تل العمارنة القديمة فكانوا يرتدون جميعا ملابس بسيطة مصنوعة من قطع كبيرة من القماش مستطيلة الشكل، مطوية ومخاطة من أعلى ومن الجانبين. وتكون فتحة إدخال الرأس على شكل فتحة طولية أو على شكل ثقب المفتاح. وعند العمل في الحقول، كان الرجال يرتدون النقبة (نوع من الملابس الداخلية ذات الشكل الثلاثي). أما الأطفال الصغار فكانوا لا يرتدون أية ملابس في الأشهر الدافئة. وعندما يبلغون سن الثامنة، فإنهم يرتدون نفس الملابس التي يرتديها آباؤهم.

كان الكثير من الناس في تل العمارنة القديمة فقراء جدا، وربما كانوا يمشون حفاة. أما هؤلاء الذين كان باستطاعتهم شراء أحذية فقد كانوا يرتدون صنادل مصنوعة من الجلد، وأوراق النخيل، والحشائش.

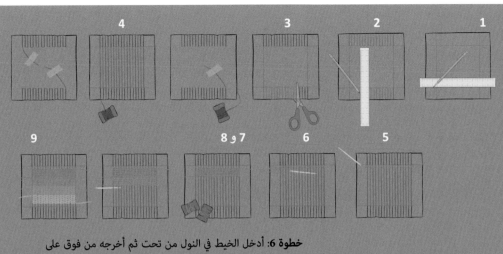

خطوة 6: أدخل الخيط في النول من تحت ثم أخرجه من فوق على نمط غرز السراجة. قم بعمل الغرزة من خلال إدخال الخيط من تحت الصف الأول وفوق الصف الثاني، وهكذا حتى تصل إلى الطرف المقابل للنول. اسحب الخيط من خلال ترك حوالي 5 سم في النهاية. ادفع الخيط لأعلى النول نحو الفتحات.

خطوة 7: أعد الخيط مرة أخرى من خلال النول من الجانب الذي خرجت منه للتو. هذه المرة سوف تقوم بعمل غرزة عكسية مقارنة بالصف الأول. يعني هذا أنه يجب أن تبدأ الخط الثاني فوق الخيط الأول إذا كنت أدخلته من تحت، أو أن تبدأ الخط الثاني تحت الخيط الأول إذا كنت أدخلته من فوق. استمر في النمط من تحت إلى فوق أو من فوق إلى تحت حتى تصل إلى الطرف المقابل للنول. اسحب الإبرة لكن لا تشد الخيط حتى لا ينحني النول! ادفع الصف الثاني من الخيط لأعلى للقاء الأول.

خطوة 8: استمر في إضافة صفوف جديدة عن طريق تبديل الغرز (من فوق إلى تحت والعكس) ولا تنس دفع الخيط لأعلى حتى يمسك كل خيط بالآخر.

خطوة 9: إذا نفد الخيط أو كنت ترغب في إضافة لون جديد، يمكنك إضافة خيط جديد. اترك ذيل على جانب من النول عند انتهاء الخيط. وعلى الجانب نفسه، أضف اللون الجديد تمامًا كما فعلت في الخطوة 6. تأكد من أنك تواصل عمل الغرزة الصحيحة وتواصل النسيج كالمعتاد.

خطوة 10: بمجرد أن تملأ النول الخاص بك، يمكنك ربط النهايات الفضفاضة من خلال ربطها مرة أخرى داخل النسيج بضعة سنتيمترات داخل الجانبين اللتين صنعتهما من خلال ترك 5 سنتيمتر من الخيط في نهاية كل صف. ثم مرر الخيط مرة أخرى إلى الخارج، اسحبه برفق وبإحكام واقطع باقي الذيل.

خطوة 11: لإنهاء النسيج الخاص بك، أزل الشريط من خيطك الأصلي في الجزء الخلفي من النول وقم بفكه من الفتحات. ادفع النسيج لأسفل على الحلقات السفلية بقدر ما تستطيع. الآن لديك حلقات علوية أطول. اقطعها في الوسط واربط الطرفين معا بدقة. وأخيرًا، اربط الطرفان الطويلان، اللذان تم لصقهما في الجزء الخلفي من النول بدقة، إلى الغرزة الأقرب وقم بوضع الطرف داخل النسيج كما في الخطوة 10.

انت انتهيت الآن! فماذا سوف تفعل مع المنتج النهائي الخاص بك؟

نشاط 10: زيارة تل العمارنة

مصر هي مقصد سياحي شهير للغاية، حيث يسافر ملايين الأشخاص من جميع أنحاء العالم لزيارة البلاد كل عام. ومعظم السياح لا يذهبون إلى تل العمارنة وهذا يعني أنهم يفوتون الفرصة لاكتشاف التاريخ المدهش للموقع ومقابلة أشخاصه المعاصرين.

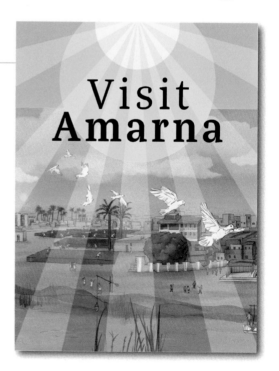

سؤال السياحة

هل يمكنك التوصل إلى فكرة لجذب السياح لزيارة تل العمارنة؟ ربما يمكنك تصميم ملصق أو منشور يحتوي على معلومات سياحية توضح ما هو مميز في تل العمارنة. ربما يمكنك التفكير في شعار جذاب لجذب انتباه الناس. قد ترغب في وضع خريطة توضح موقع تل العمارنة في مصر. يمكنك أيضًا إضافة بعض النصائح حول السلوك الجيد في المواقع الأثرية لمساعدة الزوار على الاعتناء بتل العمارنة أثناء زيارتهم . قد يتضمن هذا أشياء مثل "من فضلك لا ترم القمامة أو تمشي على الأنقاض". هل يمكنك التفكير في أي نصائح أخرى لحماية الموقع؟

مسرد

بردي: مادة تشبه الورق السميك مصنوعة من جذع نبات البردي

بعث: الولادة من جديد، مثل الحياة بعد الموت

تخمير الجعة: نشاط عمل الجعة

تسجيل: عندما يتم كتابة شيء ما أو رسمه أو تصويره

تميمة: شيء صغير، مثل قطعة من المجوهرات، يعتقد الناس بقدرته على الحماية من الحسد

تقزم: حالة تسبب أن يصبح شخصا ما قصير القامة بصورة غير عادية

جيل: فترة من الزمن مدتها حوالي 30 عاما تفصل بين أشخاص من أعمار مختلفة، مثلا طفل وأم وجدة هم ثلاثة أشخاص من ثلاثة أجيال مختلفة في نفس الأسرة

حاشية: مجموعة من الأشخاص حول شخص مشهور يعتنون به ويلبون احتياجاته

خزف: مادة زاهية الألوان ولامعة (تشبه الزجاج قليلا)، وغالبا ما تكون زرقاء

دف: آلة موسيقية، مثل طبل صغير بشخاليل على الجانبين تهزه أو تضرب عليه بيديك

دليل: شيء ما يمكن الحصول على معلومات من خلاله، مثل أغراض قديمة، مبان أو نقوش

ري: توجيه الماء إلى النباتات لمساعدتها على النمو

زخارف: تصاميم فنية غالبا على شكل أنماط

سترة: ملبس بدون أكمام يغطي الجزء العلوي من الجسم، مثل تي شيرت طويل أو فستان

سخام: المسحوق الأسود الذي يخلفه دخان النار

سد: حاجز يتم بناؤه على نهر ليحجز المياه خلفه

صوامع: المباني المستديرة المستخدمة لتخزين الحبوب داخل مخازن الحبوب

طقوس: أفعال يتم تأديتها بنظام ثابت كجزء من ممارسات دينية أو أية احتفالات أخرى

طيات: ثنيات للتزيين في قطعة ملابس

عجين: خليط سميك من الدقيق والماء يوضع في الفرن فيصبح خبزا

فطريات: نبات بدون زهور أو أوراق خضراء، مثل الفطر أو العفن

قرابين: الأشياء التي يتم تقديمها لشخص ما، تشبه الهدايا، مثل الطعام الذي يُترك للآلهة كجزء من عبادة دينية

كاتب: شخص وظيفته كتابة ونسخ الوثائق

كبسولة زمنية: حاوية تحتوي على عناصر من فترة زمنية معينة

كتان: قماش مصنوع من ألياف نبات الكتان

كفن: قطعة من القماش يُلف فيها الميت لدفنه

كلت: ملبس شبيه بالتنورة التي تصل إلى الركبة

محاجر: الأماكن التي يتم فيها حفر أو قطع الحجارة من الأرض

متماثل: عندما يكون نصف التصميم منعكسا على النصف الآخر، مثل الصورة في مرآة

محظور: ممنوع

مخازن الحبوب: الأماكن التي يتم تخزين الحبوب فيها

مشرفون: الأشخاص الذين يشرفون على الآخرين، خاصة العمال

معماريون: الأشخاص الذين يخططون ويصممون المباني

مهجور: عندما يُترك شيء ما أو يتم التخلي عنه

موقد: مدفأة

مكتف ذاتيا: الشخص الذي ينتج كل ما يحتاجه

نقبة: قطعة قماش صغيرة يتم ارتداؤها كملابس داخلية

نول: إطار يُستخدم في نسج القماش

الوزير الأعظم: المستشار الأعلى للملك، مثل رئيس الوزراء حاليا

مع السلامة!